# THE COMPLETE BOOK OF
# EVENTING

# THE COMPLETE BOOK OF
# EVENTING

## JANE HOLDERNESS-RODDAM

CHANCELLOR
PRESS

First published by Hamlyn.
This edition published in 1996 by Chancellor Press
an imprint of Reed Books
Michelin House
81 Fulham Road
London SW3 6RB

© Reed International Books 1988

ISBN 1 85152 934 9

Publisher's note:
All of the photographs were taken by Bob Langrish with the
exception of the following: those on pp. 16-17 and 48-49,
which were taken by Sandra Langrish.

Colour artwork by Eugene Fleury
Illustrations by Roger Coleman
Cartoons by Anni Axworthy
Diagrams by Brazzle Atkins

Printed in China

# CONTENTS

# INTRODUCTION

Eventing is the most varied of all equestrian sports. It comprises dressage, in which a series of set movements is performed from memory in an arena; cross-country, where the competitor jumps a course of solid and imposing fences at speed; and show jumping, in which a single round of coloured fences is jumped. Scoring is on a penalty basis and the lowest score at the end of all three phases is the winner.

There are different levels of the sport, basically consisting of novice, intermediate and advanced standard (although some countries may have different names). Most of these events take place over one day and are called a one-day event; however, these really serve as the stepping stone to the ultimate test – the three-day event. It is the ambition of all serious eventers to do one of these.

The three-day event, of which the Badminton and Burghley Horse Trials are the most famous in the world, places great demands on horse and rider. The care, preparation and training required to produce a horse that is mentally and physically well prepared for the challenge is quite daunting, but the rewards are endless and eventing has enjoyed growing popularity over the last decade.

The second day, known as the speed and endurance section, plays by far the biggest part. It includes two phases of roads and tracks and a course of steeplechase fences, followed by a compulsory 10-minute halt and veterinary inspection. All this happens before the cross-country, making the whole distance covered on the second day somewhere in the region of 10-15 miles. To compete at this level demands knowledge and considerable experience of both the riding and stable management of competition horses. This book aims to help you make a start in what is one of the most varied and challenging of all equestrian sports.

To be successful, a partnership must be built up between horse and rider and, while there are all sorts of criteria which could be considered ideal, the main aspects are a genuine, sound, willing, and well prepared horse with a dedicated, fit and enthusiastic rider.

Confidence is vital and this must be built up between both parties during their preparation. If this is lacking it is very difficult to really get a partnership going, so a little time spent getting the basic points right will pay dividends later on.

Because of its all-round nature eventing is a great 'fun' sport – a type of equestrian pentathlon. You don't have to be brilliant at any particular phase – just good enough at all three to compete successfully. It goes without saying, however, that the better you are the more successful you will become. After all, success is really what sport is about.

*Jane Holderness-Roddam*

Jane Holderness-Roddam.

The author and Gelert of Wales; Badminton, 1986.

6

# TEAMING UP
## WHAT TO LOOK FOR

**1**

Eventing is a sport for the versatile rider and the horse, too, needs to be a good all-rounder.

The majority of people probably already have a horse and decide on eventing as a natural progression from cross-country or jumping. If you are going out to buy a horse specifically to event, however, there are several factors which should be considered.

### What to look for

First of all, consider the sport. It is tough and rugged, so aim for a hardy type of horse which will be able to cope with this. The dressage phase is judged on performance and paces, so an attractive horse with good movement and a temperament to remain calm in the dressage arena is likely to appeal to the judges.

*Temperament* is particularly important, as this is a sport where calmness and the ability to relax become more vital as you progress up the ladder. A sensible approach to life without getting too over-excited sounds relatively straightforward, but it is often difficult to find a horse that possesses these qualities.

*Jumping ability* is an obvious requirement, but the horse must have the scope to be able to jump a variety of fences. It must be just as easy for him to pop over little awkward obstacles as it is to gallop on over the big, straightforward ones. The horse therefore needs to be athletic and strong and to have the ability to gallop, and yet be able to twist and turn over the jumps.

*Conformation* is very important in theory,

**A good type of event horse: deep through the girth, with straight, strong legs and good feet.**

although many good event horses have come in all shapes and sizes. Bear in mind that the legs and feet have to take a lot of strain. Straight legs with good joints, hard clean tendons and well-shaped and shod feet at least mean you are starting off well.

A good sloping shoulder usually ensures flowing movement. This is important, as a straight or 'stuffy' (coarse) shoulder is an indication that the horse may not be able to gallop very well and will have a rather choppy stride. This type of movement means the horse will take quite a lot of strain on his front legs. A good back end with strong quarters and second thigh is of great importance in many people's opinion. This is where the power comes from, so strength here is certainly an advantage. Strong hocks and back complete the picture.

*Size* depends very much on the rider. While the ideal is probably around 16.00 to 16.2 hands high, the important point is that the horse suits the rider. A tiny person on a huge horse is not usually the ideal combination, as someone short having to control a strong, galloping 17.00 hander coming into a combination fence at the end of a course is rarely a good idea. Having said that, there have been numerous instances where a large horse has been just as successful as one of 15.00 h.h. – the smallest size eligible to compete. The make and shape are what counts; for the galloping and speed elements you do not want too heavy a horse, nor a 'weed' with little bone and breadth. The latter, however, should not be confused with the 'wiry' sort who are often as tough as old boots, nimble as a cat and able to go on for ever.

Eventers seem to come in all shapes and

sizes and on looks alone few would probably have been chosen. The age of the horse plays a big part in forming your choice. A young horse is a challenge and everything is wonderful if all goes right. Ask yourself, however, if you could cope if it did not. Have you got an experienced person to help you with training? Would you be better learning the sport on a more experienced horse and then bring on a young one? Most horses are not ready to start eventing until they are six years old, although the rules allow five-year-olds.

In the final analysis, you get a gut feeling whether you like the horse or not. The character and the eye are two of the most important factors, and if these are particularly attractive to you then you will probably overlook other minor faults.

When choosing your horse
see how he reacts to you as
a rider as this may give you
an early indication of his
temperament and how well
he is likely to adapt to
different people and
situations. Mark Phillips and
the aptly named Classic
Lines; Badminton, 1984.

Everyone has different likes and dislikes but it is important to have the horse vetted to ensure that physically he is all right for the job and that he is clean in heart, eye, wind and limb. Only a professional can tell you that you are at least starting on an animal that is basically sound.

## Insurance

This is always worth considering. You can arrange this quite simply, but do choose a reputable firm with a good name. You can insure for various problems such as death from whatever cause, theft, straying, and loss of use, in which you can normally keep the horse but get a percentage of the money if it becomes unsuitable for eventing because of injury. Veterinary fees can be very expensive when things go wrong. Most insurance companies will cover tack also, and if you have a trailer rather than a horsebox do ensure this is actually covered as well as the towing vehicle. If in doubt, ask someone with experience in this field to advise you on what would be of most benefit to you in your particular circumstances.

## Stabling

Having got your horse organized it is imperative that he is kept in suitable conditions. These do not have to be palatial but must be of adequate size, warm, well-ventilated and safe. Check carefully to ensure there are no protruding nails or other sharp objects; horses have an amazing capacity to find such things and injure themselves. Electric cables, wires and sockets must be kept away from where the horse can chew them. Paddocks and fields should be well fenced and regularly checked, and have water available at all times. All horses benefit from being turned out, even if it is just for a short time daily. If you have only limited grazing, keep this fresh by picking up the droppings regularly; cows or sheep would clean up the grass. Rest the paddock periodically and add fertilizers, if necessary.

## Schooling facilities

These are essential in some form. Many people do not have an arena or ménage but are able to find something locally which they can use.

Although dressage can be practised in the field you will be governed to some extent by the weather and the ground conditions. Fitness work can be carried out on roads (if they are safe) and along tracks, bridleways and through woods; hills are one of the best ways of fittening a horse, so take full advantage of these. Neighbours with land are usually very helpful so long as you respect their ground and only use it sensibly. There is no doubt that horses do make a mess in wet weather and whether it is your own or someone else's land you need to apply a little common sense in such conditions as to where you ride and what you do.

It is easy enough to make an arena for dressage if you have a nice flat area. Upturned buckets make good markers and it is easy to paint the letters on them. While a large area is fine for schooling, it is worth riding at times in one the correct size for your test. Make your arena 20×40 metres so that you can practise your dressage movements and perfect them. This is the correct size for Novice and Intermediate tests in Britain but at Advanced level the larger arena of 20×60 metres is required. Arenas can be marked out by using string, pegs and a patient friend!

You'll need some practice fences and poles. Your bare minimum should be at least six uprights and eight poles. Fillers can be made up of a variety of bits and pieces, but in all cases make sure they are safe. Tyres from the local garage are easily come by and you can make a variety of fences from these.

Painted poles are bright and colourful. If you have a young horse you will have to accustom him to these and you should ensure there are several different colours and patterns so that he will not be alarmed by them in competition.

Cross-country fences may or may not be available to you, but it is important to school over these occasionally, particularly if you have a young horse. Between them, your riding friends will usually come up with some fences locally. It is, however, quite a good idea to have a few built at home – a couple of ditches of different sizes are useful as you can place poles before, after or over them to vary the effect.

Water can sometimes be found nearby in the form of a river, stream or pond and, once you have made quite sure the bottom is safe, the more your horse gets used to it the better.

## Transport

A horsebox or trailer for travelling completes the major essential requirements. Nowadays there is every kind of vehicle available; many have living accommodation, which makes such a difference if you have to stay overnight. What sort you have is a matter of personal preference, but make quite sure there is ample room for your horse first and foremost. Check the floor carefully (and continue to examine it regularly) and make sure there is adequate space for your kit. Whether you opt for a trailer or horsebox, everything must be safe and easy to manage so establish that you can cope single-handed with the opening and shutting of ramps, doors and partitions – inevitably there will be times when help with these is not available.

Be sure to look at how your horse is expected to get in and out of the vehicle. Two ramps are a definite advantage, but if this is not practical do be quite happy that your horse will be able to negotiate whatever type you choose without injury or stress.

If you are looking for a non-heavy goods vehicle check that it really is in that category. Make sure that all paperwork is legal and that you have relevant MOT/plating certificates etc.

The above are all the major requirements for eventing and these, along with tack, travelling kit and the necessary rugs and rollers, represent quite a major outlay. Fortunately all the equipment, if looked after, lasts well and has a good second-hand value if you find it necessary to change anything at a later stage.

---

## GOOD VIBRATIONS

'Finding the right horse is a vibe in a funny sort of way. Very occasionally I get on a horse and feel at one with him – it happens, but extremely rarely. I particularly like a horse that is aggressive and can do his own thing.' – *Lucinda Green, six times winner at Badminton*

# BUILDING UP

## THE BASICS

**2**

When you embark on getting any horse into condition it is most important that you attend to the basics when the horse comes in from grass and starts work.

### Feet and legs

Shoeing is probably one of the most important single factors for the event horse. Because of the nature of the sport, the legs and feet get considerable wear and tear and regular shoeing, paying particular attention to the shape of the foot, is essential if undue strain is not to be put on the feet and tendons. Studs are a tremendous asset in slippery going so ensure your farrier knows when you require these.

Watch your horse's legs and really get to know them. The legs are the vital link in the event horse and it is essential that any signs of trouble such as heat or swelling are noted and assessed immediately before any further damage is caused. A few days spent in quiet walking will pay dividends at the crucial time should there be any question of a problem. A gallop could break a horse down if there is some underlying trouble, so make it a daily routine to feel the legs morning and night before deciding on your horse's exercise.

### Veterinary routines

The teeth require attention once or twice yearly and regular checks should be carried out to ensure that there are no rubs or sores in the mouth. Have your vet rasp the teeth before they become a problem. Sharp teeth often affect the horse's way of going and cause evasions in the mouth, as well as affecting how well he can eat.

Worming is necessary every 6–8 weeks and must be conscientiously carried out. There are many wormers on the market today which are effective against all the main debilitating worms, including red worm and lung worm, and it is worth discussing the merits of each with your veterinary surgeon before embarking on a regular programme.

Vaccinations against tetanus and equine flu should be kept strictly up to date. In many places you will be unable to compete without your 'flu vac' and different countries have their own recommendations. Do not overwork your horse for at least a week after he receives his

*Early schooling helps build up muscle and strength, but must not be over-done with the young horse. Here, horse and rider look happy in their work even though mother appears to be stamping her foot!*

injections or, if possible, arrange for the vaccinations to be given during a period when he is resting.

### Feeding

Feeding, a highly specialized subject, is really the secret of success. Your horse must be given the right food in order to perform well and yet remain sensible enough to do the job required of him. A well-balanced diet goes without saying, but amounts depend very much on the type of work being done. Modern feeds now have most of the essentials included in some form or other, especially in cube or coarse mix formulations.

Remember the golden rules of feeding – feed little and often, and water before meals (although most horses nowadays have water freely available). Make any changes in the diet gradually over a period of several days. Feed according to the work being done and always provide the best quality foodstuffs – in particular, have good hay.

Study your horse regularly to see that he is coming up to shape. A fit horse should not be too fat; he should have a good top line and be lean without being thin, so as not to put any undue strain on heart, lungs or limbs.

As the horse's work increases you should increase its energy feed and decrease the bulk feeds. Good quality hay should be fed on a regular basis, depending on your horse's make and shape, as the horse is naturally a grazing animal and should always have something to pick at except for a few hours before galloping. Very greedy horses may require a little given at intervals during the day. A bran mash with salts given once or twice weekly before a rest or easy day aids the digestive system by its slightly laxative action; it helps to clear the rather concentrated modern foodstuffs through the stomach

and reduces the risk of a build up of protein and stasis in the limbs over a day off. Epsom salts, added at least once a week, keep the system free of any build up of unwanted deposits in the blood.

Horses all have different habits, but it cannot be stressed too strongly how important it is to keep all feed mangers and water buckets clean. Dirty mangers accumulate stale food round the edges and can quickly put a sensitive feeder off.

Some horses have a slight dust allergy which causes them to cough, so give these individuals fairly damp feeds and soak the hay for several hours. This is usually best done by placing the haynet in a large, clean, plastic dustbin and filling with water. Tip out the water and drain the haynet for half-an-hour before you give it to the horse as it will weigh a ton! This method will usually cure any cough problems but if not, then vacuum-packed hay may be the answer.

Boiled feed is very palatable and good for fattening horses but, because of this, should be used with caution when the horse is in full work. It is excellent given after a hard 'work day', as it is easily digested and very warming in the cold winter months. It is best soaked for a few hours before being boiled then cooked in a slow oven overnight or until soft. Allow it to cool sufficiently before feeding.

There are numerous supplements on the market which all claim to benefit your horse in various ways, but a horse which eats a well-balanced diet, looks healthy, is good in his coat and bright in his eye should not really require any extra. Very often a supplement will tend to unbalance the diet and have the opposite effect to that promised. However, some horses may need extra help so choose one that seems right and stick to it, having first checked with your vet that there is no underlying cause hindering your horse's condition, such as anaemia caused by a virus, an infection, bad teeth or worms.

### Grooming

General stable care includes regular grooming, which not only keeps the horse clean but stimulates circulation and, with strapping, increases muscle tone. This helps towards producing a supremely fit and well-prepared horse. Pay particular attention to keeping your horse warm

### OPPORTUNITY KNOCKS

'There is much more opportunity to get through in eventing nowadays compared to when I competed. There are many more events to train at and bring a horse on.' – *Margaret Hough, Badminton winner, 1954*

## HORSE TRIALS

'The event horse needs a good temperament: to be as brave as a lion as well as sane and sensible. He also needs to be fast enough to win a race. We riders spend our lives trying to find the best way of producing a horse capable of fulfilling these criteria.' – *Clarissa Strachan, European team medallist*

and out of draughts – the fit horse may be easily chilled and suffer back stiffness if he is left standing in a draught, so change rugs as necessary during the day if the weather suggests it.

## Work at the walk

You should start work in ample time to ensure that the horse will have a fair chance of getting to his first event of the season in good shape. A build up of work at the walk commences when the horse is first brought in after a rest period. Walking is accepted as the best method of hardening legs and generally toning up muscles. Three quarters of an hour, increasing to up to 1½–2 hours by the end of the second week, is a rough guide. Start by just quietly walking your horse, making sure he walks out and does not slop along. After the first week you can add interest to your rides by sometimes asking for a lengthening and shortening of the stride or by practising halts.

In Britain we tend to do quite a lot of road work to harden the legs, but this should only ever be done at a walk or a slow trot. Trotting fast merely jars the legs – the slow work is what builds up and hardens muscle and helps to increase the elasticity in the tendons. In our soft going this becomes very important to avoid the risk of strains. In America, Australia and other countries where the ground is in general much firmer, care should be taken not to do too much on the firm ground.

If you are lucky enough to be able to work up hills you can save hours of time, as this will be far more beneficial than work on the flat. Not only will it help to build up muscle power but it will also increase lung performance and save on fast work later on in your build up programme.

## FITNESS PROGRAMMES

### 1. For a horse coming in after a long rest

| | |
|---|---|
| Week 1 | Road work – walking. Start 45 minutes, increase to 1¼ hours per day by end of week. |
| Week 2 | Road work – walking. 1–1½ hours daily. Hold horse more together in between periods of stretching. |
| Week 3 | Road work – walk and introduce periods of slow trot. |
| Week 4 | Road work – walk and longer periods of trot. 1¼– 1½ hours daily. |
| Week 5 | 30 minutes road work and 20 minutes schooling three times a week. Road work or hack on other days. |
| Week 6 | 1 hour road work or hack out daily. Schooling daily. Grid work – 1 session. |

### 2. For a horse coming in after a short break (2–4 weeks)

| | |
|---|---|
| Week 1 | Road work – walking. Start 1 hour, increase to 1½ hours by end of week. |
| Week 2 | Road work – walk and slow trotting or little schooling. |
| Week 3 | Hack out and 30 minute schooling sessions. 1 grid session. |
| Week 4 | 30 minutes schooling and hack out. 2 grid sessions. 1 canter. |
| Week 5 | Hacking out and 30–40 minutes schooling. Cantering. 2 grids. |
| Week 6 | Hacking out and schooling. Cross country practice or 1 gallop. |

### 3. For a horse returning to work after a long lay off following tendon injury

| | |
|---|---|
| Weeks 1–4 | Road work, walking only – 45 minutes increasing gradually to 2 hours. |
| Weeks 4–6 (or 8) | Road work walking, introducing slow trot. |
| Week 6 (or 8) | 30 minutes road work. 10 minutes schooling, gradually increasing, 2–3 times a week. |
| Week 8 (or 10) onwards | Follow Chart 2 as from Week 3. |

All horses to have a day off once a week being led out to graze or, if sensible, turned out.

How long you continue with slow work depends on whether the horse is totally unfit and starting from scratch, has just had a short break from work or has had an injury. Whatever the case, remember that all work should be increased gradually and in most cases a two-week period of walking is essential before embarking on the more serious schooling. If you are bringing your horse back into work following

an injury a much longer period of walking should be adopted so that the leg can harden up thoroughly before any other strain is imposed on it. When planning your build up programme keep this in mind and add an extra fortnight to allow for any unforeseen injury.

## Slow trotting

The next stage is the gradual introduction of slow trotting. As trotting increases so periods at the walk become fewer but always walk after any steep hills and avoid the severest ones until your horse is fit enough to cope with them. You must never strain your horse during this crucial time. Generally speaking, this period could also last for two weeks but make sure the horse is really working and don't allow him to become idle. Make sure that he has breaks from being held together and is allowed to stretch his neck at regular intervals in between.

## Schooling on the flat

Once this initial two-stage period is over you should feel confident that the horse has been given a good start and schooling on the flat can now be introduced. Some people like to hack first and then do a bit of schooling daily, others prefer to school first; either way is fine, so long as you start with a good 10-minute period of walking on a loose rein to loosen the horse up. Remember that a few short sessions are much better than one long one and be careful not to overdo these early schooling stints. Avoid too many really small circles and work on establishing a rhythm and making the horse obedient.

As the horse fittens up he may become a little playful and care is sometimes necessary to ensure that you keep him obedient and under control. Every horse is different and you should always be alert to the unexpected — some are very relaxed about life, others far too exuberant for their own good.

Jumping is best left until the horse has been in work for at least a month to six weeks, depending on what he has done. Grid work (see p. 30) is the best schooling for the event horse. It teaches him to think and become more alert, and generally to learn to be more athletic — so essential if he is to become a safe conveyance across country.

The eventer needs to be a hardy animal to cope with the obstacles in the cross-country phase. Slow, steady work to build up good, hard tendons is essential if this sort of fence is not to strain the horse's legs; Hilary White and Contrast, Pony Club Horse Trial Championships, 1987.

# LEARNING PRECISION

## SCHOOLING

Dressage or basic schooling is essential if you are to be successful. The word dressage tends to sound rather daunting, but in essence what is required is obedience from the horse to perform your demands with ease and willingness.

This will not be possible unless the horse is supple and has been correctly and sufficiently trained to perform set movements in the dressage arena. The horse needs to learn to stay in balance and to be able to go in straight lines as well as on the circle in all paces. This sounds simple enough but few can get the best from their horses on the big day, so perfection at home must be aimed for in the hope that at least some of this will show through at the event.

### Schooling the rider
Before you get the best from your horse, you must ensure that you are getting the best from yourself. First and foremost, dressage is about riding well, and to be able to ride well your position must help rather than hinder the horse.

If your head and upper body tend to get too far forward it will be difficult to be in an effective position to drive the horse forward. Lungeing the rider is one of the best methods of achieving a good position and the emphasis must be on creating a firm seat and leg and supple, still and relaxed arms. With the stirrups removed, the rider must work on gaining a firm but supple seat in the saddle as the instructor works on different exercises to accomplish this. Arm exercises will loosen the shoulders, waist and elbows and these will also help with balance and a firmer leg position. It is essential that the instructor is always in full control of the horse during a rider's lunge lesson and that a suitable horse is used. A quiet, preferably enclosed area

is the ideal situation. There is always a tendency for the rider to draw upwards when riding without stirrups instead of relaxing down into the saddle and this is one of the most important points to be worked on. If it is not possible to have someone lunge you and tell you where you need to improve, then riding at home without stirrups will be beneficial anyway. Remember to let your legs and seat sink into the saddle, allow your waist and upper body to grow taller and hold your head up. Do not allow your body to lean in on the turns or circles but always stay straight and upright in the saddle.

### Schooling the horse
Schooling should be done regularly to help build up muscle, balance and ability. Start with a loosening up period on a long rein and gradually get the horse together, pushing rather than pulling it into an outline but being sure to find the right level for that horse's rhythm and balance.

At this stage it does not matter greatly if you don't have a proper schooling arena. A good surface is the most important aspect and whether this is in a field or not is immaterial so long as you can work consistently in that area. If riding in a field, avoid making tracks as these invariably tend to leave marks and the ground becomes very dead and slippery in the wet.

Work the horse little and often with periods of walking, allowing and encouraging him to lower and stretch his neck muscles as often as possible. Work on establishing a good rhythm by creating the right degree of balance between your hand and leg for the horse to achieve this. Practise straight lines and keep the horse moving forward well so that he has the balance to be able to do this, as well as working on the circle.

Change the pace as often as possible and increase and decrease at walk, trot and canter to help the horse carry himself. The use of your leg here will enable him to do this with ease if you employ it correctly. Be sure to vary the movements, as going round and round an arena does little good to anyone – it is the exercises you perform that will improve the horse. Do suppling exercises in the form of a serpentine, starting with three loops where the bend must be changed as you go over the centre line each

---

**BALANCING ACT**

'Dressage is the art of balancing your horse for the corners and on the circles and during the increase and decrease of all paces. This is of prime importance and makes such a difference when balancing before taking a fence.' – *Jennie Loriston-Clarke, Novice Championships winner*

Each year it is becoming more important to gain that head start over other competitors by doing well in the dressage phase. The standard worldwide has improved tremendously in all phases so if you are too far behind after the dressage it becomes very difficult to catch up, however brilliant you may be at cross-country or show jumping; Bruce Davidson and J.J. Babu, Badminton, 1985.

time. As the horse progresses so can the exercises – it will soon become clear when he is ready to do something a little more advanced, such as a four or five loop serpentine. Loops off the track and back on again help balance and co-ordination and these can be varied in many different ways.

To perform any movement the rider must prepare the horse in plenty of time and create more energy by stronger use of the leg and seat to collect the horse. This extra energy can then be released into the movement required. For medium paces in walk, trot or canter the horse is pushed strongly forward to take a longer stride. In extended work this is exaggerated even more with the horse lowering his head a little and being pushed forward to extend his stride to his maximum. The balance and control is maintained through the rider's hand and leg. It is important to keep the rhythm and not to overdo

Master Craftsman is showing slight tension in his mouth, but is trying hard and being kept in balance through Ginny Leng's legs, hands and seat; Stockholm, 1987.

# LEARNING PRECISION
## LEG YIELDING/SHOULDER-IN

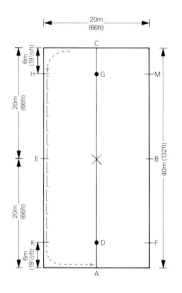

The shoulder-in is performed down the side of the arena for most event tests. The shoulders are brought to the inside of the track and the horse looks away from the direction in which he is travelling.

There are four main movements required for horse trial dressage tests at the different levels. These are leg yielding (which is fairly common in the US but is not used in Britain or Australia), shoulder-in and half pass in trot, and counter canter.

### Leg yielding

This movement is the simplest as it is basically asking the horse to move away from the leg. The horse's body is straight except for a slight bend at the poll away from the direction in which he is moving. The rider will therefore see the horse's inside eye only. The inside legs will cross the outside legs as the horse is pushed forwards and sideways by the rider's strong inside leg pressure. Collection is not required for this movement, which has prompted some trainers to question its value as a test. However, it is used inevitably in all forms of training, wittingly or unwittingly, as the rider has to ask the horse to move away from the leg when he opens or shuts a gate or to avoid a hazard.

### Shoulder-in

The shoulder-in is the most widely used suppling exercise. The horse moves forwards, bent very slightly from head to tail round the rider's inside leg and looking away from the direction in which he is travelling. This movement can be performed in straight lines or on the circle to create extra suppleness, as the inside hind leg has to increase its flexing action to perform the movement. The rider must maintain the straightness of the movement by preventing the quarters from swinging out and keep the bend by controlling the shoulders. First start practising in walk and then progress to trot. To do shoulder-in the rider is best starting the movement after coming out of a corner and should bring the forehand in from the track and increase the inside leg to keep the bend. The outside leg will prevent the quarters swinging out (see illustration). The hands control the movement with the inside one maintaining the bend and the outside one controlling the angle. The horse should be on three tracks with the inside foreleg on the inside track, the inside hind leg and outside foreleg on the middle track and the outside hind leg on the outside track. The

the exercise, particularly in the trot, until the horse has really learnt to remain in balance. Otherwise he may either break into a canter or hurry the pace rather than lengthen the stride.

### THE MOVEMENTS

In lateral work the horse moves sideways at the same time as going forwards and is bent slightly either towards or away from the direction he is going. At all times the forward motion must be maintained. The secret of success with all lateral work is to maintain an even rhythm and this can only be achieved if the horse is adequately balanced and collected to be able to perform the movement (except for leg yielding). Be careful not to hurry your horse as he will need time to organize himself into the movement. Over-pushing may result in evasions such as tail swishing, grinding of teeth and general unhappiness about the job in hand.

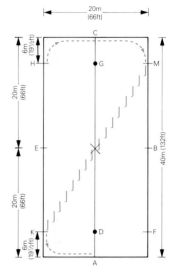

The half pass is performed across the arena. The horse's body should be almost straight with the legs crossing and the horse looking in the direction in which he is travelling.

degree of angle should never be more than to allow the three tracks. If you feel the horse labouring then straighten him a little and ask again with less angle.

## Half pass

The half pass is the most advanced and impressive of the lateral movements. The horse moves diagonally across the arena with the forehand just very slightly in advance of the hindquarters. The outside legs cross over in front of the inside legs and the horse is looking and bending uniformly throughout his body in the direction in which he is travelling. The half pass for eventing tests is only asked for in trot.

It is usually best to start after a corner or 10-metre circle and push the horse back towards the opposite track, maintaining the bend in the direction he is going. Do this by keeping hold of the inside rein and softening the outside one towards the direction you are going. Keep the outside leg behind the girth, pushing the horse over in the direction you are travelling with the inside leg on the girth keeping the forward movement. You must sit up and look in the direction you are travelling.

Problems are usually caused by the horse not going forward enough and losing impulsion and rhythm, and either leading with or trailing the hindquarters. This can be corrected through more leg and a re-balancing of the horse before asking him to move sideways again.

## Counter canter

Counter canter is an excellent suppling exercise and is basically used to maintain rhythm and balance. It is found in the most advanced tests. The horse is asked to lead with the outside instead of the inside foreleg and so canters on the 'wrong leg'. He requires enough impulsion

# LEARNING PRECISION

## COUNTER CANTER

**Above:** The counter canter is a balancing exercise whereby the horse remains on the same leg even when changing direction. The rider must maintain an even feel with the hand. There are various sized loops and serpentines expected in tests at Intermediate and Advanced level. The illustrations show the movements for a 3-loop serpentine (see diagram). The counter part of the movement is shown in light blue.

to stay cantering on the 'wrong leg' and the secret is not to shift the weight but keep the balance throughout on the outside hand. The horse should be collected up to shorten his stride and then asked for loops of up to 8–10 metres off the track and back on again.

Start by doing very shallow loops and gradually increase these. Do not swing the body but keep upright and maintain an even contact throughout on the outside rein so that the horse can keep his balance. Once the horse is used to this, large circles, serpentines, etc, can be performed, but only ask for more bend if the horse's canter is short and collected enough between the rider's hand and leg.

Problems are usually caused by shifting of the weight or asking for too tight a circle with insufficient collection and a loss of balance. Some half

halts or re-balancing through greater use of leg into hand should cure this, along with paying particular care to maintaining the weight. If you have problems maintaining the canter, practise shortening and lengthening the stride on the straight and then return to the movement and try again.

### The tests

Learn the movements required in a test but do not always do these in the correct sequence. The horse may start to anticipate if he has done things too often, so vary all movements frequently. If an exercise is not going well it is often better to change to something different and then come back to that movement rather than have an argument – which rarely does any good in the long run anyway!

### VYING FOR THE EYE

'Dressage is a chance to show off one's paces, not only the horse's!' – 'Tiny' Clapham, Olympic silver medallist

Most Novice tests will be looking for the way the horse performs circles – usually between 10–20 metres wide – and for his ability to lengthen and shorten the stride in all paces.

At Intermediate (called Preliminary in the US) level a little more is expected and tests with 10 metre circles, medium and working walk, trot and canter paces, shoulder-in or leg yield, halts and rein backs may all be introduced, as well as counter canter loops and simple changes.

In Advanced tests lateral work is expected in the form of shoulder-in, leg yielding and half pass, more advanced counter canters such as three-loop serpentines and more emphasis on movements performed in collected and extended paces.

Riding a test is quite an art, as it re-

The halt should be square with both front and hind legs opposite one another.

It is important to ride in an arena of the same size as that in which you are going to ride your test. There are two arena sizes (see diagrams): the small (pp 22-3) is 20×40 metres and the large (above left) 20×60 metres. In Britain, Novice and Intermediate tests are performed in the small arena with the Advanced in the large one; in the United States the large arena is used for most tests. Learn to know where the letters are in both arenas. The basic quarter and half markers are the same for both arenas and form the sequence AKEHCMBF – most people memorize these with their own little saying (mine is All King Edward's Horses Cannot Manage Big Fences). RSVP fills in the gaps in the large arena. DLXIG completes the centre line. X and G are the only ones you need to know for most tests, being where you halt at the beginning and end.

# LEARNING PRECISION

## THE TESTS

**TYPICAL NOVICE STANDARD TEST**
**To be ridden in snaffle bridle**

Max. marks

| | | | |
|---|---|---|---|
| 1 | A | Enter at working trot* | |
| | X | Halt, Salute. Proceed at working trot | 10 |
| 2 | C | Track right | |
| | B | Circle right 20m diameter | |
| | BFK | Working trot | 10 |
| 3 | KXM | Show a few lengthened strides | |
| | M | Working trot | 10 |
| | | Between | |
| 4 | M&C | Working canter left | |
| | C | Circle left 20m diameter, on returning to | |
| | C | Round the arena to A | 10 |
| 5 | A | Working trot | |
| | B | Circle left 20m diameter | 10 |
| 6 | HXF | Show a few lengthened strides | |
| | F | Working trot | 10 |
| | | Between | |
| 7 | F&A | Working canter right | |
| | A | Circle right 20m diameter, round the arena to C | 10 |
| 8 | C | Working trot | |
| | M | Medium walk | |
| | B | Half circle right 10m diameter to L | |
| | | Half circle left 10m diameter to E | 10 |
| 9 | K | Working trot | |
| | A | Down centre line | |
| | G | Halt. Salute | 10 |
| | | Leave arena at walk on a long rein at A | |
| 10 | | General impression, obedience and calmness | 10 |
| 11 | | Paces (freedom and regularity) and impulsion | 10 |
| 12 | | Position and seat of the rider and correct application of the aids | 10 |

TOTAL   120

*All trot work for novice tests may be executed either 'sitting' or 'rising'*

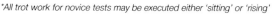

laxed and proficient approach by the rider to get the best from the horse in the atmosphere of an outing. This is not always easy, especially in the surroundings in which most events are held. The horse can often see and hear the show jumping and cross-country and if he is the type that gets excited on such occasions you do have a bit of a problem.

Accuracy is important and lack of this is an unnecessary way of throwing away marks. Each new movement should start as your body

The extended trot is one of the most elegant movements in the dressage test. The immaculate turnout of horse and rider add to the general overall impression of the performance; Torrence Watkins-Fleischmann and Finvarra; Badminton, 1985.

## THE TESTS/TACK

**TYPICAL INTERMEDIATE STANDARD TEST**
**To be ridden in snaffle or double bridle**

|   |   |   | Max. marks |
|---|---|---|---|
| 1 | A | Enter working trot* | |
|   | X | Halt. Salute. Proceed at working trot | 10 |
| 2 | C | Track left | |
|   | E | Circle left, 10m diameter | 10 |
| 3 | A | Down centre line | |
|   | C | Track right | 10 |
| 4 | B | Circle right, 10m diameter | 10 |
| 5 | A | Halt. Rein back 4 steps. Proceed at medium walk | 10 |
| 6 | KXM | Change rein at free walk on a long rein | |
|   | M | Medium walk | 10 |
| 7 | C | Working canter left (directly from walk) | 10 |
| 8 | E | Circle left, 15m diameter | 10 |
| 9 | A | Half circle left, 20m diameter to X | 10 |
| 10 | X | Simple change of leg and half circle right 20m diameter to C | 10 |
| 11 | B | Circle right, 15m diameter | 10 |
| 12 | A | Working trot | |
|   | KXM | Change rein at medium trot | |
|   | M | Working trot | 10 |
| 13 | HXF | Change rein at medium trot | |
|   | F | Working trot | 10 |
| 14 | A | Down centre line | |
|   | G | Halt. Salute | |
|   |   | Leave arena at walk on a long rein at A | 10 |

Collective marks

| 1 | Paces (freedom & regularity) | 10 |
|---|---|---|
| 2 | Impulsion (desire to move forward, elasticity of the steps, suppleness of the back and engagement of the hindquarters) | 10 |
| 3 | Submission (attention and confidence; harmony, lightness and ease of the movements; acceptance of the bridle and lightness of the forehand) | 10 |
| 4 | Position, seat of the rider, correct use of the aids | 10 |

TOTAL 180

*All trot work for intermediate tests is executed 'sitting'

The double bridle should always be comfortable and well fitting.

passes a marker, so remember to prepare the horse a little beforehand. Obvious changes of pace are vital so that the judge is quite clear what you are attempting and a definite difference needs to be shown between working, collected, medium or extended paces.

Smoothness and maintaining a balanced rhythm throughout are other factors which help towards success. Dressage is a visual art; it should be pleasing to the eye and the horse must be schooled to be able to perform all movements with ease.

The rider must memorize the test and be confident of the sequence of movements. Practise riding the test until it becomes second nature, so that you can concentrate on producing a competent performance. Be careful, however, that you do not do this too often on the horse which will be competing as he may memorize the test himself and start anticipating, which then makes it very difficult to ride a good test.

### Tack

Tack for dressage varies slightly according to the standard of test, in that for Novice tests snaffle bridles only are allowed but in Intermediate or Advanced tests the simple double bridle may be used. Different countries have slight variations in their national rules and you should always make a careful check to ensure you have a 'legal' bit or noseband. There are many different snaffles that may be used but whereas a 'French' snaffle is allowed, the rather

# THE TESTS/TACK

**The snaffle with flash noseband.**

similar 'Dr Bristol' bit is forbidden. Most nosebands, grackle (crossover) and a flash as well as cavesson and drop may be used, but remember that this is not the case if you are in a pure dressage competition where, in Britain anyway, grackles (crossovers) are forbidden.

Few people have a saddle for each phase of eventing but the straight cut dressage saddle does encourage a better position for the dressage phase. The longer leg required is more likely to be achieved in a saddle correctly cut for this than the forward cut of the jumping saddle which tends to encourage the rider to sit further back with the leg too far forward for dressage.

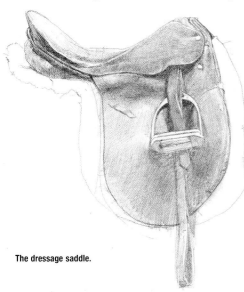

**The dressage saddle.**

**TYPICAL ADVANCED STANDARD TEST**
**To be ridden in snaffle or double bridle. Spurs are compulsory**

Max. marks

| | | | |
|---|---|---|---|
| 1 | A | Enter at working canter | |
| | X | Halt. Salute. Proceed at working trot* | 10 |
| 2 | C | Track right | |
| | MXK | Change rein at medium trot | |
| | K | Working trot | 10 |
| 3 | P | Circle left 10m diameter | 10 |
| 4 | BG | Half pass left | |
| | C | Track left | 10 |
| 5 | HXF | Change rein at medium trot | |
| | F | Working trot | 10 |
| 6 | V | Circle right 10m diameter | 10 |
| 7 | EG | Half pass right | |
| | C | Track right | 10 |
| 8 | M | Extended walk | |
| | MXK | Change rein at extended walk | |
| | K | Medium walk | 10 |
| 9 | A | Halt – rein back 5 steps – Proceed at working canter left, without halting | 10 |
| 10 | AC | Serpentine 3 loops, each going to the long side of the arena. The first and third true canter, the second counter canter | 10 |
| 11 | HXF | Change rein at extended canter | 10 |
| 12 | F | Working trot | |
| | A | Working canter right | 10 |
| 13 | AC | Serpentine 3 loops, each loop going to the long side of the arena. The first and third true canter, the second counter canter | 10 |
| 14 | MXK | Change rein at extended canter | |
| | K | Working trot | 10 |
| 15 | A | Down centre line | |
| | G | Halt. Salute Leave arena at walk on a long rein at A | 10 |

Collective marks

| | | |
|---|---|---|
| 1 | Paces (freedom & regularity) | 10 |
| 2 | Impulsion (desire to move forward, elasticity of the steps and engagement of the hindquarters) | 10 |
| 3 | Submission (attention and obedience, lightness and ease of movements, acceptance of the bridle) | 10 |
| 4 | Position, seat of the rider, correct use of the aids | 10 |

TOTAL  190

*All trot work for advanced tests is executed 'sitting' unless stated otherwise

29

# JUMPING

## GRID WORK

The most important part of eventing concerns the jumping phases. Cross-country riding is exhilarating at any time, but nothing is more exciting than galloping through the finish at the end of a good round over big and imposing fences.

The show jumping phase requires precision and accurate jumping. So often competitions are won or lost when a fence is knocked down, losing a valuable 5 points. A single pole can mean the difference between a win or nowhere, so it is most important that this part of the event is treated with due respect.

With the emphasis now being placed on rather trappy and twisty courses it is imperative that the event horse learns how to cope with every type of problem and is able to perform whatever the weather or state of the ground. Training should be planned with this in mind.

### Grids

Grids are one of the best ways of making a horse more athletic and supple and of teaching it to think and look after itself. These are made up of a variety of poles and fences set at different heights and distances. To start with, grids should be quite simple and gradually build up according to the horse's ability and degree of training. Start by using a line of trotting poles to get the horse used to seeing them. These can be spaced at between 4–5 feet, depending on the horse's stride at trot, or at between 9–10 feet, in which case the horse can trot a stride in between the poles or canter through them.

After a couple of exercises introduce a small cross pole and then a pole 9 feet away to encourage the horse to look down and to round his back over the fence. After he has done this twice, introduce another cross pole 9–10 feet further on. This can be repeated until there are four or five jumps interspersed with poles. Grids can be varied in all sorts of ways. The longer your grid the more space you should allow between obstacles. It is important that the distances are right for your horse and that he achieves what he is being asked to do.

The young and inexperienced horse must be started over simple fences. Cross poles encourage neatness in front, while parallels make for a round jump. The poles on the ground are useful to make the horse look down, so encouraging a good bascule (rounding) over the fence.

Vary the fences as much as possible to get the horse used to the many different types and change some fences so as to have one stride to one fence and two or three strides to another. Poles on the ground instead of fences will help to keep the horse in balance and concentrating.

Grids increase a horse's balance and athletic ability. It is best to start with trotting poles and then gradually introduce jumps. Vary the distances between poles and between jumps to teach your horse to think for himself and adjust his stride as necessary, but make sure that each grid is within his capability. Build up in easy stages and don't confront him with too much at once. Below are shown two simple examples.

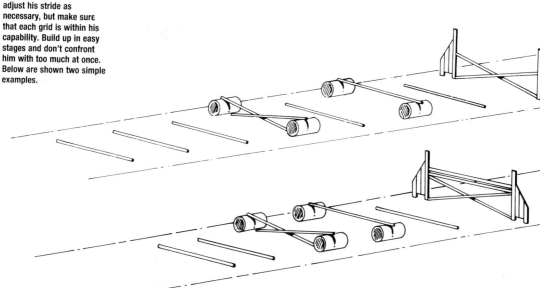

The jumper needs to be neat and this horse has really raised his forelegs well to clear the fence. He is also using his head and neck nicely. The rider is in balance with him despite her lower leg having slid back too far; Lorna Clarke and Glentrool, Badminton, 1986.

# JUMPING

## *THE TECHNIQUE*

*1.* The rider drives the horse forwards towards the fence. Notice how the horse lowers his head as he approaches the fence.

*2.* Raising the forehand on take off.

## The technique

Jumping is a natural movement for the horse but man expects an extremely athletic and balanced animal to be able to perform accurately over fences in a confined area. Man's expectation requires a good deal of skill on the part of the rider to help the horse perform successfully. The essential requirement is for the rider to remain in balance, keeping his weight lightly but securely over the horse's centre of gravity so as not to interfere with the action of jumping.

You should shorten your stirrups by a couple of holes for jumping to give yourself a greater angle from hip to knee to ankle. This will allow you more flexibility as your weight should be kept just out of the saddle with your knees and ankles acting as shock absorbers during the action of jumping. The hands should follow the head movement, allowing the horse as much rein as he requires.

There are five main phases to concentrate on when jumping: the approach, the take off, the moment of suspension, the landing and the recovery (see illustrations).

The approach is the most important part to get right. If this is correct the subsequent phases should cause no difficulty. The horse must be going forward confidently (**1**). He should be straight, balanced and maintaining a steady rhythm with his hocks well underneath him so that he is able to spring into the air. You must keep your lower leg against the horse with the weight well down into your heel. Sit forward, following the horse's movement, and keep a quiet but consistent feel on the reins. As the horse nears the fence he will lower his head to prepare for take-off. He will then rebalance by shortening his neck, raising his head as he lifts his forehand off the ground (**2**). He will fold up his forelegs and spring into the air from his hocks. You must fold forward from the hips in time with the horse, keeping a flat back, your head up and your weight evenly distributed square above the horse. Your heels must remain firmly down in the stirrups while your legs lightly grip the horse. Slide your hands forward as the horse stretches his neck (**3**).

During the moment of suspension (**4**) the horse should round his back, bringing his

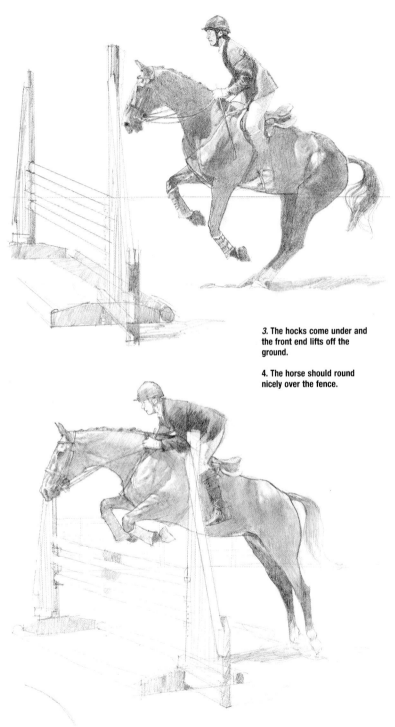

**3.** The hocks come under and the front end lifts off the ground.

**4.** The horse should round nicely over the fence.

# JUMPING

## *THE TECHNIQUE*

withers up so that for a split second they are the highest point and lowering and stretching his neck forward and down while tucking up all four legs close to his body. Give the horse as much rein as he needs by sliding your hands forward further. Sometimes it will be necessary to open your fingers and 'slip the reins' to allow the horse a little more freedom of movement, particularly if he has made an awkward jump. Remain forward during this period with your weight just out of the saddle.

As the horse prepares to land (**5**) he will straighten his forelegs and start to shorten his neck and raise his head in order to rebalance himself. Raise your body more upright and shorten your arms to maintain the balance. Slightly brace your legs forward, but maintain the forward impulsion and keep your weight down in the heel.

To recover his stride (**6**) the horse brings his hocks well underneath him so that he can prepare for the next fence and be balanced for whatever comes next. The impulsion and rhythm must be re-established immediately as the rider prepares for the next fence. Ensure that you are back in normal jumping position as the horse gets into his stride. There should be no 'bump' back into the saddle on recovery. A 'bump' indicates an unbalanced landing, which could unsettle and worry your horse for subsequent jumps.

*5. The front legs stretch out and the horse's head starts to lift as he balances himself for the landing.*

*6. The pick up for the next stride should be neat and set horse and rider smoothly on their way.*

### Practising

This should be done once or twice a week, but not overdone. If the horse has done some grid work regularly he should have learnt how to be neat and quick-thinking, which will be enormously helpful when he comes to the cross country where he will often have to think for himself in order to get out of trouble. Remember that for the cross-country he should be capable of 'jumping a bounce', so this should be incorporated into your grid occasionally. Some fences need jumping at an angle, so to make sure that your horse is not surprised by this practise jumping from both sides on the angle and line another jump up to complete a double on the angle.

Jumping single fences from trot and canter, popping over them quietly and turning in off the track or out on to it will help to build up a partnership as both horse and rider will learn how each reacts and so will gain more trust in one another. It is this mutual confidence that is so important and that makes for a really good partnership.

Riding up and down hills is extremely beneficial, not only in increasing balance but also for fittening the horse and strengthening muscles. Some horses will handle a hill with ease; others get totally unbalanced, but the more they do the more they will improve. Avoid really steep hills on the whole, and work up and down gentle slopes trying to maintain a rhythm.

### Show jumping

This is the most specialized type of jumping which requires great accuracy. Once your horse has done the initial training and learnt to respect fences and how to handle them you must put thought and practice into the art of riding a show jumping course. The horse will need the experience of jumping plenty of coloured fences so that colours and patterns are of little conse-

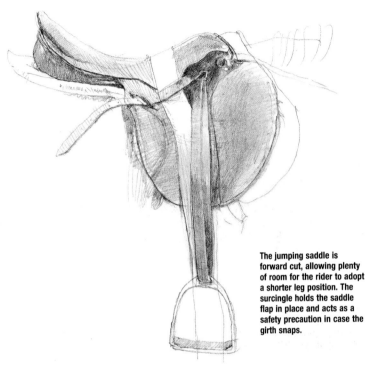

The jumping saddle is forward cut, allowing plenty of room for the rider to adopt a shorter leg position. The surcingle holds the saddle flap in place and acts as a safety precaution in case the girth snaps.

quence and he must be quite confident that he can cope with so many jumps in a confined space. Doubles and trebles should hold no terrors for him and it is with these fences that the gridwork will have helped so much. A combination of jumps and a mass of coloured fences could be a daunting prospect to many horses, but those that have done gridwork will have learnt how to assess such situations and will approach them with confidence.

Walking the course and working out where the problems are is an art only learnt with years of experience, but the importance of a straight approach to each jump cannot be overstated. To achieve this is sometimes difficult, especially when coming off a turn, but aim to give the horse the best approach possible so that he and you have time to concentrate on clearing each obstacle.

Look at the course as a whole and consider how to make the most of it. Check if there are related distances involved between one fence and another and, if so, get your line sorted out in

### AGONY AND ECSTASY

'90 per cent of anything to do with horses is sheer unadulterated hell, but the other 10 per cent makes up for it.' – *Helen Ogden, British international rider*

The rider is in an excellent position over this cross-parallel. There is a nice straight line from the elbow, through the hand to the bit, and the leg position is firm. The crash hat with safety harness is compulsory for cross-country and show jumping; New Zealand Olympic rider Andrew Bennie and Gray Shot, Gatcombe, 1987.

# JUMPING

## SHOW JUMPING/CROSS-COUNTRY FENCES

An open ditch needs to be taken boldly. This rider has met the fence just right and is all set for a lovely ride over it. Both horse and rider look confident and happy – which is always a good sign! Elinor Hannay and Final Touch; Windsor, 1986.

your mind and keep the same rhythm and pace to meet this correctly. Vertical fences such as gates, planks and walls need accurate riding. Parallels require a bit of extra impulsion but not necessarily speed.

Take the above points into account as you walk the course, and be certain you are clear about the start and finish lines and have appreciated any awkward turns which could affect how you get to a certain fence. A clear round is what you are aiming for and your course must be assessed with that firmly in your mind. If possible ascertain what your bell sounds like so that you are not left wondering which of the many strange noises usual at an event is possibly your start signal.

The warm up practice fence should be used as that and no more. Far too often one sees disasters in the collecting ring as anxious competitors are panicked into practising over a fence that has been adjusted to suit the requirements of others and is far too big. The end result is often a horse and rider totally demoralized just at the time they require maximum confidence!

Before attempting your practice fence warm your horse up on the flat. In cold weather it is even more important to do this really thoroughly as muscles will not work properly until they are loosened up.

A cross pole is probably an ideal warm up fence for everyone. It is relatively small and is best approached in trot. A vertical followed by a parallel may be all your horse requires. Some horses do not 'open up' as well as they might, but a slightly wider parallel should achieve this. Keep the pace and rhythm coming into the fence and concentrate on what you are doing in spite of the melée around you. If you have any

problem make it a rule to immediately lower the fence before retaking it, and be very positive next time you jump it.

If possible always have a helper with you to alter fences as there are invariably some that are much higher or lower than you require; the reason why so many people frighten their horses in the collecting ring is that they are tempted to jump what is already there rather than starting off correctly.

### Cross-country fences

These come in all shapes and sizes, and familiarization with the many different types and knowledge of the technique required to jump them is essential if mistakes are not to be made. Grid work will once again have been of enormous benefit in teaching the eventer to think for himself and cope quickly with whatever type of combination he is facing.

The main point to remember when riding across country is that you are riding fast over solid fences and therefore *every* fence needs treating with respect to negotiate it safely. The pace should be controlled and even throughout. While it needs to be fast enough to negotiate the fences with ease it must also be practical, depending on the going, type of course and the horse's ability to get round within or close to the time.

The different types of fences can probably be broken down into the following: uprights, spreads, banks and steps, combinations, water, ditches and fences with lids on.

*Uprights* (**1**, see page 40) should cause few problems so long as you do not get too close and you appreciate the siting of them and how this will affect your jump. Notice whether the fence is imposing and solid looking (these usually jump well) or rather small and flimsy (these often do not jump well). Has it a false groundline which could encourage the horse to get far too close and hit it, or is it a nice straightforward fence? These thoughts and more should pass through your mind. In bad going always check on how the fence will look should you want to jump to one or either side of the centre, which could become deep and boggy by the end of the day.

*Spreads* (**2**) should generally be ridden at with

# JUMPING

## CROSS-COUNTRY FENCES

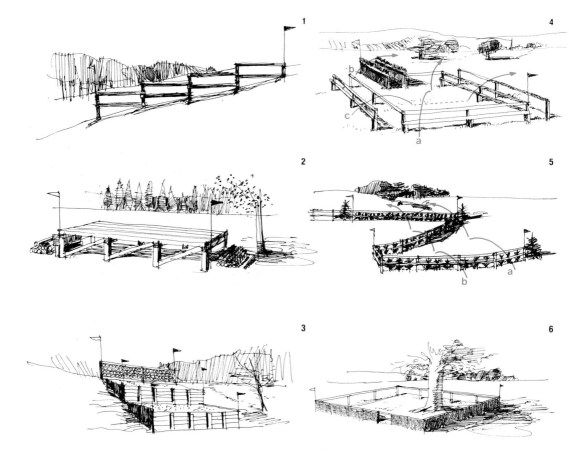

plenty of impulsion, without encouraging the horse to stand off too far and thus making them unnecessarily wide. Sloped spreads jump beautifully but parallels must be treated with a bit of respect to ensure the horse clears the first rail cleanly. Hold the horse together well between hand and leg without losing too much pace.

*Banks and steps* (**3**) require great impulsion, particularly when jumping up on to them. They should always be ridden straight and the forward movement maintained regardless of whether you are going up or down. If there is a jump off, keep riding the horse forward so that he does not land too deep over the drop. Do not go too fast over steps down or straight drops off banks as this will tend to jar the horse and he

may not want to go so willingly over the next one.

*Combinations* (**4-6**) come in a huge variety of different designs, but all require some balance and preparation for a controlled approach so that you meet your planned line through the fence exactly right. 'Bounces' need even greater control to get the horse back on his hocks enough to jump these neatly. 'Corners' (**6**) can be taken very often in preference to an in and out (see **5**), but get your line absolutely right. You must, when walking this, choose a spot past the fence with which you can line up on your approach. Aim for the safe spot (see illustration **5**), which is relatively small at these obstacles, and ride strongly forward into the fence. 'Coffins' (**7**) are a classic combination fence and

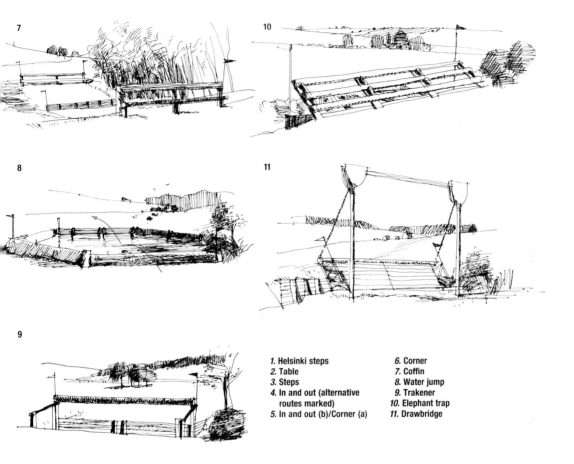

**7**

**10**

**8**

**11**

**9**

1. Helsinki steps
2. Table
3. Steps
4. In and out (alternative routes marked)
5. In and out (b)/Corner (a)
6. Corner
7. Coffin
8. Water jump
9. Trakener
10. Elephant trap
11. Drawbridge

consist of rails, a ditch (sometimes two) followed by rails again out. These may or may not include a slope down to the ditch and it is the degree of slope and the closeness of the component parts that determine the difficulty. They require very controlled riding but also plenty of impulsion, and the rider must remain in balance so as not to hinder the horse by getting out of position.

*Water* (**8**) is either jumped over or into and needs some thought if mistakes are not to be made. To jump over an open water, water ditch or water with a pole on top etc. the horse needs riding on and the fence treated much the same as a sloping parallel. Jumping into water requires a balanced, controlled approach and the pace will very much depend on the depth of water, degree of drop and size of the fence.

Generally speaking it is best to approach slowly at a bouncy canter or strong trot then ride on strongly. You need to encourage the horse to jump out well and not pitch too much over the drop as it is during the next stride after landing when the 'drag' of the water is at its greatest that the crucial stage is reached. Sit up well and support the horse with the hand throughout the negotiation of the water.

*Ditches* (**9-10**) cause a lot of excitement and consternation among the riders but usually pose relatively few problems if ridden correctly. The golden rules are 'never look down into a ditch' but 'ride forward over one' and this is really the secret to it. Ditches in front of a fence may appear a little spooky but act as a nice take off rail; they require strong riding forward. A

# JUMPING
## CONDITIONS/PROBLEMS

**Most problems are solvable and many of those that do occur where horses are concerned emanate from the rider. These three cartoons are gentle reminders of the traits that every aspiring eventer should guard against. I hope they speak for themselves!**

ditch after the fence is rarely seen by the horse but should be ridden on at to ensure he jumps out. Tiger traps and rails over a ditch again need strong riding.up and over – make sure the horse does not slow down to look too hard but is kept firmly going forward.

*Lidded fences* (**11**) are now becoming much more common and seldom cause trouble. Some horses, however, do tend to duck their heads when going through this type of fence and then fail to get their legs up high enough to clear it well. You must really get the horse together and make him concentrate on the fence rather than the lid, so ensuring you get a good clean jump. The horse will flatten a bit if he ducks his head so hold on to it well to support him.

### Conditions
The going will make an enormous difference on how a fence jumps. A straightforward fence may be transformed into quite a difficult one if the going becomes slippery and you must appreciate that in boggy ground the horse will actually be required to jump much bigger as he sinks into the mud. The extra effort required in these conditions means the horse will need more pace going into the fence to compensate.

Very hard slippery surfaces are also a nightmare, as not only are you expecting the horse to jump on very jarring ground but you are also hoping that he will be neat over his fences. Few horses are going to want to jump really big ob-

stacles in these conditions and, if at all possible, will avoid jumping them altogether.

The use of studs will improve the situation. Large ones are generally used behind and small in front. In very hard ground small sharp pointed studs may be best all round as the other kind will not make much impression on really hard going.

Some horses feel lost in bad going and tend to lose confidence unless they have studs, while others seem quite unconcerned and require them only occasionally. A lot depends on how balanced and well ridden they are as to how they cope with the different going.

### Problems
When training a horse you will inevitably come up against problems, whether schooling for the show jumping or cross-country phases. The horse may stop, run out or continually knock a fence. The rule here is analysis. It is usually the rider's fault when things go wrong, so begin by examining what you've been doing and why it has caused a problem. Are you expecting too much of the horse by presenting him with fences that are too ambitious for his stage of training? Are you getting into the wrong position and so making everything too difficult? Your weight may be too far forward in the saddle; you may not be giving the horse enough rein over the fence; or perhaps you're giving him so much that there is loss of contact – and therefore balance – between horse and rider. Is the horse

in pain for some reason – corns, a strain, sore mouth, a back problem? It may be that he's suffering from a virus or some other illness. When you've worked out the root of the problem, waste no time finding a remedy. If the problem stems from faulty riding technique, enlist the help of a more experienced person to coach you out of it. It is easy to develop bad habits which could seriously undermine your and your horse's confidence, thus jeopardizing your development as a team.

Working out why things aren't going to plan is the most difficult part of solving any problem, whatever it is. Putting matters right is usually fairly obvious though rarely quick or painless, so be patient and prepared to persevere.

Occasionally you may come to the point where you realize that perhaps your potential eventer just simply does not wish to be one, however carefully you have done all the initial work. Like humans, animals do not always conform to the model we have in mind for them; very often all goes well until they reach the point that is as far as they are willing or able to go in that sphere. They may, however, be brilliant at one aspect of eventing and so become a star as a show jumper or dressage horse instead.

# SAFETY FIRST
## PERSONAL EQUIPMENT

The saying 'it is better to be safe than sorry' is a wise one and very apt when used with reference to eventing. There is always an element of danger involved in something that requires riding at speed, in this case over solid fences. It is not necessarily when in the saddle that accidents may occur – you can just as easily be kicked or bitten when you have two feet on the ground – but a fall certainly looks very dramatic. It is in everyone's interests to minimize the risks and take as many precautions as possible.

### Personal equipment

A *riding hat* is the most important and essential item. At no time should the rider be on a horse without one, but it is no good wearing one unless it fits and will stay on. There are various types on the market, but you should only ever choose one that conforms to the official safety standard. Always wear your hat with the harness correctly adjusted so that it remains firmly in place should a fall occur. The importance of a well-fitting hat, correctly adjusted so that it stays on, cannot be over emphasized.

Even for everyday riding, you should always wear suitable *footwear*. Riding boots or jodhpur boots were designed for the purpose and even the rubber ones, although hot, come up to expectations and are shaped to fit when you are in the saddle. Hats and boots are the two main essentials for riding.

*Gloves* not only protect the hands but in some cases also have a non-slip action. This is very useful, particularly if you are jumping, when the horse will tend to sweat a lot. Leather gloves on

plain leather reins may well become too slippery so they should be avoided or used only with rubbered or other non-slip reins. String or 'pimple' gloves are excellent as non-slip everyday gloves.

Many people wear a *back protector* for jumping and this is a wise precaution. There are various designs and which you choose is a matter of personal preference. They should always be worn when riding across country. Some designs are extremely hot, so try them out to see which you find the most comfortable.

*Stocks or hunting ties* are essential for cross country. They have prevented many a serious injury by supporting the neck and protecting it from scratches and bruising. They are correct dress for all three phases in competitions.

*Whips and spurs* are used for all phases but make sure the spurs are blunt and incapable of wounding your horse. The buckle should be fastened on the outside with the leather 'points' facing downwards (see illustration). Whips need to be easy to hold without them slipping through the fingers. Elastic bands looped round the top

**Wearing a back protector is a wise precaution and has prevented many nasty injuries. There are many different varieties on the market. This type is reinforced down the spine and is held in place by an elasticated strap.**

### KEY TO SUCCESS

'Safety in any sport is of the utmost importance. Eventing is no exception. Hard hats, back protectors and constantly "checked" equipment all help to prevent unforeseen accidents.

'We all suffer falls – not only on the cross-country! At the risk of sounding like a head-mistress, safety is the key to happy eventing.' – *Virginia Leng, Current World and European champion, and Olympic gold medallist*

The Normandy Bank is always a slightly daunting fence requiring a bold approach and neat jump over the post and rails with a drop landing. Jean-Paul Saint Vignes and Jocelyn A appear to be having a good jump and look set for a safe landing; Badminton, 1984.

## PROTECTION FOR THE HORSE

*Right:* **Whips can only be used for the cross-country and show jumping phases. Whichever type you choose to carry, it must not exceed 30 inches in length. It is wise to select one which has a broad knob at the top end; it won't be nearly so painful should you poke yourself in the eye with it! Dressage whips can be any length, but are only allowed when schooling outside the arena.**

*Below:* **Well fitting boots give good protection for all types of riding. Spurs should always be worn with the buckles on the outside and their points facing downwards.**

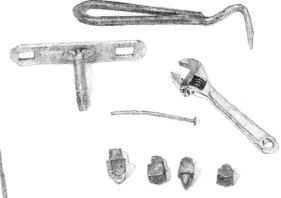

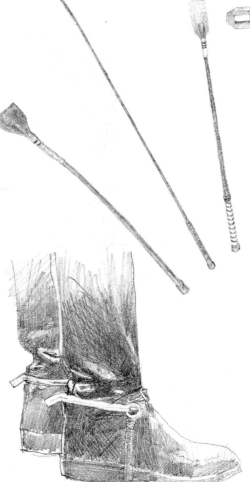

and equipment in use.

Start with the hooves. A well-shod horse will at least be given the best chance to cope with the ground, fences and type of terrain to be covered. With a tough sport demanding accuracy and surefootedness this must be top priority. Be sure your horse's feet are in good shape, that they have not been allowed to grow too long so putting an undue strain on the tendons, and that all clenches are down and the foot is smooth all round. Make it a rule to see your blacksmith regularly every three to four weeks when competing as, even if the shoe is tight, the foot will have grown and will need cutting back. A shoe left on too long could cause corns; a horse will not want to jump big fences with uncomfortable feet and will either stop or tend to crumple on landing over a big fence, possibly resulting in a bad fall. All too often there have been serious injuries caused by lack of care and foresight in this area.

*Studs* will be enormously beneficial on slippery ground. Generally, small ones are best in front and large behind, but it may only be necessary to have hind ones or small all round. Don't underestimate how slippery the dressage arenas can become, however. Do not leave large studs in for long periods if your horse is to stand in the horsebox all day. This will add an extra strain on his tendons, which is not ideal.

*Boots or bandages* will protect the legs and help prevent the everyday type of knock and

may help or, for better grip, get the type that is rubberized. Choose a whip that has a flat, smooth top to it, as it is easy to poke your whip in your eye at times when jumping and too sharp a top will not do you much good.

### Protection for your horse

As far as protection for the horse is concerned it is best to look through all the possible areas where injury could occur and then at the tack

# PROTECTION FOR THE HORSE/SADDLERY

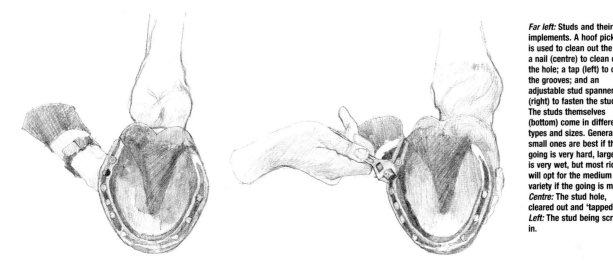

*Far left:* Studs and their implements. A hoof pick (top) is used to clean out the hoof; a nail (centre) to clean out the hole; a tap (left) to clear the grooves; and an adjustable stud spanner (right) to fasten the studs. The studs themselves (bottom) come in different types and sizes. Generally, small ones are best if the going is very hard, large if it is very wet, but most riders will opt for the medium variety if the going is mixed. *Centre:* The stud hole, cleared out and 'tapped'. *Left:* The stud being screwed in.

bruise which can put your horse out of the running. Study his action and look at his legs to see if he knocks himself regularly and if so where before deciding which form of protection would be best. Bandages can give better support but are so rarely well put on that they are more likely to cause an injury than prevent it. Boots must fit the leg and be kept scrupulously clean so that they do not cause a rub or sore. The fastenings used must be secure and have a double safety fastener, for jumping in particular. Velcro is not strong enough on its own when going through mud; either use boots with a double fastener or tape them, being sure that you do not pull the tape round the leg at a greater tension than that of the boot, as this could cause pressure on the tendon. Bandages should be evenly and firmly applied and must protect the joints. They should be stitched in position and any loose ends cut off or taped at the same tension as the bandage.

Over-reach or bell boots will help to protect the heels from being struck by the hind feet. There are various sorts on the market, with the pull-on variety remaining the best even though they are awkward to use. Be careful of any design that has the buckle low down as the horse could tread on it, causing him to stumble or fall.

Many riders use *grease* down the front of the hind legs and over the knees for cross-country. The point of this is to prevent further injury should the horse get stuck on a fence or caught up anywhere as the grease will help the horse to slide off rather than injure the skin more. It is probably only necessary if the horse is likely to get tired and start to land short at his fences. A fit horse should not have this sort of problem if he is sensibly ridden, but an accident can occur at any time for any reason.

## Saddlery

The right saddlery for the job is, of course, one of the most important decisions that has to be taken. Above all it must be safe, strong and in good condition. The bridle is best made from strong, fairly wide leather, especially if your horse is a real puller. Likewise the breastplate, which should be worn so as not to hinder the shoulder movement of the horse, will ensure that the saddle does not slide back too far — quite a hazard once the horse is very fit and lean. *The saddle* must be a good fit and comfortable on the horse. If a weight cloth is to be carried you should have a good numnah underneath this. Make sure you pull the weight cloth right up into the front arch of the saddle (see page 76) before tightening the girth to prevent pressure on the withers, which could affect the horse's jumping.

*Girths* must be strong and well tightened without overdoing it. There are various kinds, but remember that broad ones are generally more comfortable. Some have strips of ribbon-type material on the outside of the main girth. Beware of these for cross-country, as they create an uneven pressure and have been known to cause a haemotoma (blood clot) which has then meant the horse being out of action for some time.

An *overgirth or surcingle* is a sensible addition. This goes on top of the saddle to hold everything in place and prevent the saddle flaps riding up. It also acts as an extra girth should the main one break.

The *bridle* must be strong and fit comfortably, with regular checks made to ensure the stitching is in good condition. The reins must be renewed as necessary and for cross-country must have some form of anti-slip assistance such as rubber covering. The right bit to give adequate control is vital for jumping. It may take some time and a little trial and error before the braking system really works on some horses but choose a bit that is the right size and width for yours.

*Running martingales* can accentuate the action of the bit and assist with steerage; they are very useful for cross country with a horse that tends to be a bit unresponsive. They can be employed by themselves or as a separate attachment to the breast plate. The reins must then have martingale 'stops' to prevent the rings from running over the rein billets and getting caught up.

The above covers most of the important side of having and using the right equipment. It goes without saying that everything must be kept in good condition, the leather must be soft and pliable and any suspect stitching should be repaired immediately.

### General safety

Other factors which involve safety concern the general preparation of your horse. A well trained and carefully schooled horse should be able to cope with the demands made upon it so long as you are not aiming too high for its level of training. Work one stage at a time and progress up the ladder only when you are quite convinced that you and the horse are ready to move on to the next phase of training.

Take your horse slowly to start with until he has the confidence and experience to go faster. Make life easier for you both by thinking ahead and getting your approaches to fences correct.

Never, ever, take unnecessary risks.

Out hacking or on the roads be alert to any dangers. If your horse is a little nervous in traffic be sure to have someone with you and make certain you can be easily seen if it is getting dark. Keep riding popular by being polite and courteous to other road users.

If you are having training problems of any form then get some experienced outside help to put it right before it becomes a habit. Likewise, don't allow your horse to get out of hand in the stable and become a danger to you or himself. He must not be allowed to kick or bite and any such behaviour should be instantly punished; do make sure, however, that there is no underlying reason for this if such behaviour starts suddenly. It could be an important indication that all is not well; injury or pain somewhere may be the cause and must be treated and cured as necessary.

Check that your stables are safe, with no sharp object sticking out on which the horse could injure himself. Any electrical wires or appliances must be well out of reach of the horse or covered. Fire extinguishers should be ready to hand and maintained in working order. Keep your first aid and veterinary kit up to date and complete with all the usual bits and pieces for dealing with minor injuries to both you and your horse.

Make sure you are training your horse sensibly and have devoted enough time to getting him fit before making greater demands of him. If in any doubt, ask someone more experienced in that particular subject to check how things are going.

As a general rule, think before you act. Never forget that patience pays dividends and that one false move may risk the hours of time you have taken to build up confidence and that very special partnership which is so essential for a successful eventing combination.

**But sometimes things go badly wrong! The usual advice if you are about to fall is 'relax'. It helps a bit if you can, but it's certainly not easy!**

> ### LION HEART
> 'Horses are all so different. They've got to be athletic to a certain extent, but they must have strength of character and be able to bounce back after a "hairy" moment.' – *Jon Evans, British international rider*

Riding in a competition is the reward which follows weeks or months of patience and hard work to have the horse at his best for the big occasion. While some competitions are used merely as schooling events in a build-up period towards something bigger, they nonetheless get the adrenalin flowing and involve just as much work to prepare properly as a more important one.

The attitude of the rider plays a large part in all competitive work. You must think and act positively and approach the whole day with confidence if you are to be of any help to the horse in the circumstances. The horse is a very receptive creature; tenseness, nervousness and a general air of apprehension are quickly conveyed to him.

Because of this it is vital that the horse and rider have full confidence in one another and achieve that special bond that grows between horse and rider and creates a partnership. While it is perfectly possible for a horse and rider to set sail successfully round a course without really knowing one another, there is little doubt that it takes time to become attuned so that your reactions to one another work the right way when there is a problem.

The partnership becomes especially important on occasions such as when you 'miss your jerk' over a big fence. This inevitably happens from time to time and the right, quick reactions to your horse's needs can save what might otherwise become a bad fall or at best a very near miss.

### Preparing your horse

Working out how your horse will need to be prepared on the day takes time and knowledge, and it helps considerably if you can understand his mentality. Is he the nervous, highly strung type, requiring hours of work to settle down before the dressage, or does he become hysterical before the jumping? Is he the type that really needs motivation to get the best from him? Maybe he comes out in the mornings feeling stiff and so rather bad-tempered. Perhaps he is the sort that can't take too much pressure and so the more you do with him the worse he gets.

How are these different types best coped with? Often it is a case of trial and error, as no two horses are the same anyway. Nervous

horses are often best walked quietly for half an hour until they really relax. If yours is the sort that won't, let him canter on a fairly loose rein for 20 minutes or so. Keep forward off his back until he settles down and you feel you can sit down in the saddle, then start working him in trot. A tense horse is usually best in rising trot and this is allowed in novice tests.

Lethargic or idle horses will usually need quite a lot of brisk trotting and cantering to limber them up before they work actively enough. Jumping them before the dressage will sometimes get them into a more sparkling frame of mind. Funnily enough, jumping sometimes works with excitable horses also. Given half a dozen jumps they start to think the day's work is over and so settle much better.

Stiff horses need quite a lot of slow loosening work. Do not exert them too much until you have really given them the chance to stretch and supple up a bit as they do need this time to be able to give their best.

The jumping phases are more difficult to cope with in competition as you are only permitted to use the set practice fences and these get horribly overcrowded with people trying to get their warm-up jump. Some horses remain calm throughout and are little problem because they will jump anything within reason. The excitable horse is best not jumping too much in these situations, but perhaps a high cross pole will make him look at the fence a little and steady up coming into it. A wide parallel should make him 'open up'; if he is quite excited don't overdo the height, but instead pop him over once or twice and keep him working in circles until you go into the ring.

Make sure you know your rules when jumping the practice fences, as some of the schooling

The end in sight – horse and rider show dogged determination as they ride to the finish of a long and tiring course. The rider's fitness is essential if the horse is to be held for those final few hundred yards; Madelaine Gurdon and The Done Thing; Burghley, 1985.

### STAYING POWER

'The wonderful thing about the sport is that many different types of horse can play the game with comparable success. It's more the adaptability of the rider that determines a rider's longevity in the sport.' – Bruce Davidson, world champion, 1974 and 1978

## CONDITIONS/DRESS/GENERAL PREPARATION

methods used at home are not allowed in the collecting ring. Be sure you only jump the fences in the right direction, with the red flag on the right and white on the left.

For the cross-country a short, sharp canter after a 5-minute warm-up and a couple of jumps to put him in the mood is all that is required before setting off round the course.

### Ground conditions

These need very careful assessment as they really will affect how your mount performs. Some horses shorten their stride on hard ground or refuse to relax for fear of slipping; others hate landing on it, and your usually fluent jumper may become a real 'propper' or start to clear everything with fractions instead of inches to spare.

Other horses get completely bogged down and feel quite unbalanced in very deep going and so are incapable of jumping well in these conditions. While practice makes perfect in some cases, it does not apply here. It is not worth the risk of asking such a horse to jump big fences in this type of ground as it will certainly undermine his confidence. Choose courses where the going is known to be good and aim your programme to avoid the wetter times of the year if possible.

### Dressing correctly

The right apparel is very important. You will give the impression of professionalism if you are always neat and tidy and look the part. There are certain accepted rules on correct dress and knowing these will stand you in good stead as you perform in front of the judges. The chart (below left) gives a general idea of what to wear for each phase at the different levels. Ratcatcher is only allowed at lower levels.

### The role of the groom

Your groom plays a very important part in your whole preparation programme as he or she is the person who best knows your horse in the stable. It is therefore very important that you work together as a team and decide between you who is to do what on the day. Careful planning always pays off and it is up to the rider to brief the helper thoroughly on the day's plans and the build up to it all. The fitness and feeding programmes must be understood and your horse studied daily, with special attention paid to his legs and shoes. A loose clench may not seem important in itself but it could easily damage the other leg.

### Checking the details

Prevention is always better than cure and risks should never be taken. In the excitement of an event it is easy to think that accidents will not happen to you but this is just when they do! Your horse may get frightened or fool around when warming up and knock himself because you have left the boots off. Do everything properly.

Do not cut corners. It may work briefly or seem cheaper but it never pays in the long run. Your horse does need first-rate hay and other food if he is to give his best. Your tack must be safe and strong, so don't adopt the attitude that something will last just one more time. It invariably won't, and one little thing like a broken leather could cause a nasty fall and cost you the

|  | Dressage | Show jumping | Cross-country |
|---|---|---|---|
| **Novice** | Ratcatcher/blue or black coat Hunting cap/bowler Hunting tie (dark with ratcatcher) Fawn/pale cream breeches Pale gloves | Ratcatcher/blue or black coat Skull cap and blue or black cover Breeches and boots Gloves | Coloured jersey Breeches and boots Skull cap and cover Back protector Stop watch Gloves |
| **Intermediate** | Blue or black coat Hunting cap/bowler White hunting tie and pin Fawn breeches and boots Pale gloves | Blue or black coat As above | As above |
| **Advanced** | Blue or black coat/ tails Hunting cap/top hat with tails White hunting tie (stock) with pin Pale cream or fawn breeches White or pale gloves Top boots | As above | As above |

competition – not to mention wasting all the time, effort and money that has gone into preparing for the event.

### Preparing yourself
Your own condition is as important as that of the horse. While everyday riding will give you a basic fitness, some extra training will be necessary if you are not to hinder your horse at the end of the course when he needs the most help. Running and swimming are the most helpful activities to increase your breathing capacity. Energetic sports such as tennis and squash are also good for overall fitness. If you have a very strong horse, press ups and arm exercises will help to improve muscle tone. Skipping, running on the spot, good knee exercises such as are used for ski-ing and plenty of brisk walking will make sure you are in good shape but do be sure to work at these activities on a regular basis.

Diet plays an important part as well and it is essential that you eat sensibly to be fully fit. Overweight people cannot ride as well as slim ones as they are the wrong shape to be able to sit and grip and remain in balance with the horse.

### Summing up
Competing is all about attention to detail and dedication to the job in hand. While you may be competing just to gain experience for the horse, get qualifications for further events. Whether you are going out to win or just for the fun of competing, you might as well do it properly. Learn as much as you can from watching others, pick out what works best for you and use this knowledge to gain the most from your sport at whatever level you are competing.

**That wonderful moment at the end of a big competition when the prize winners perform a lap of honour. For the lucky ones it makes all the months of preparation and hard work worthwhile. Though not the winner this time, Lucinda Green shows how delighted she is with Shannagh's performance; Stockholm, 1987.**

# ONE-DAY EVENT

## PREPARATIONS

Entering for your first one-day event of the season is an exciting moment, giving a feeling of anticipation that after the weeks of training and fitness work the ultimate goal is in sight at last.

Make quite sure you have studied the entry procedure. It can be a fairly long winded affair and, as the sport increases in popularity, the chance of being balloted out also rises. Entry forms that are not correctly and legibly filled in will automatically be discarded, so it is in your own interests to get it right and to send it in by the set date.

Read your Rule Book carefully before the start of the season so that you are aware of any changes which might affect you or your horse and you have thoroughly understood anything which might concern your participation in the class. Learn how each phase is run, the scoring system and, in particular, the penalties given at the various types of multiple fences if you do not aim for the quick bold routes (see table below). It is easy to make mistakes in the heat of the moment but be sure that you do not cross your track when negotiating combination fences (see diagram right).

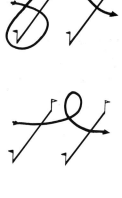

**Right: Methods of incurring penalty points at combination fences. Any of these faults will cost you 20 penalty points.**

### Preparation

The preparation for the big occasion is vital and the importance of careful planning of your day cannot be overstated. If necessary make out lists of equipment required for horse and rider and don't forget to include hay, food and water for the horse to cover the journey to and from the event.

If you are stabling away take mucking out tools and night rugs as well as water and feed buckets and a hay net. Find out whether you need to bring your own straw, shavings or whatever.

Check that your vehicle is full of fuel, that the water and oil are topped up and that tyres are in good condition and of the correct pressure – this can affect the way your horse travels, particularly if you are using a trailer.

Pack everything (after ensuring it is clean) in the order that you will need it. The equipment checklist on p. 56 may prove a useful guide.

### Arriving at the event

Allow plenty of time to get to the event and, if staying overnight, to settle in. Find out where everything is situated and how to get easily to each different site. If it is hot try to get the box

### PENALTIES FOR THE CROSS-COUNTRY PHASE

| | |
|---|---|
| First refusal, run-out, circle of horse at obstacle | 20 penalties |
| Second refusal, run-out, circle of horse at same obstacle | 40 penalties |
| Third refusal, run-out, circle of horse at same obstacle | Elimination |
| Fall of horse and/or rider at obstacle | 60 penalties |
| Third fall of horse and/or rider | Elimination |
| Error of course not rectified | Elimination |
| Omission of obstacle or boundary flag | Elimination |
| Retaking an obstacle already jumped | Elimination |
| Jumping obstacle in wrong order | Elimination |
| For every commenced period of 3 seconds in excess of the optimum time | 1 penalty |
| Exceeding the time limit | Elimination |

Water is one of the obstacles that demands great respect. Once safely in, it pays to steady up a little to give the horse a clear view of what he is expected to do on the way out; Mary Crawford and Red Gregory, Pony Club Championships, 1986.

## CHECKLIST/DRESSAGE PHASE

### EQUIPMENT CHECKLIST

#### FOR HORSE

**Travelling**
Leg bandages or wraps
Tail bandages and guard
Sheet (or rugs) and roller
Headcollar and rope
Knee caps – hock boots if used
Bedding (if necessary)

**Feed**
Water and carrier
Feed (all necessary kinds)
Salt and/or electrolytes, if necessary, to prevent dehydration in hot weather
Hay
Buckets and feed bowl plus scoop

**Tack**
Saddles – dressage and jumping
Bridles for each phase if necessary
Girths
Breast plates
Numnah and spares
Weight cloth and weights if required
Over girth/surcingles
Over-reach boots
Boots/bandages plus tape

**General**
First aid kit
Mucking out kit
Grooming kit
Fly spray
Waterproof sheets
Anti-sweat rugs and coolers

Buckets, sponges and scrapers
Studs and tools
Tack cleaning kit
Spare set of shoes
Lungeing kit
Spare headcollar and rope

#### FOR RIDER

**General**
Hats for each phase (and hair nets)
Coats (ratcatcher or black as required)
Gloves – light coloured and non slip
Shirts
Hunting tie/stock or pin-tie
Boots and garters
Spurs – dressage and jumping
Whips

**For cross-country**
Sweater
Stop watch
Card for writing times if required
Spare gloves
Back protector

**General**
First aid
Course walking shoes
Rule book
Times and schedule
Wet weather gear
Spare clothes
Food and drink
Clothes brush etc.

### The dressage phase

The day starts with the dressage phase. Warming up for this is very important and you must not underestimate the amount of time your mount will need. Your lovely quiet horse working obediently at home may become quite ridiculously naughty or uptight at the event, so unless you know exactly how he is likely to react give yourself plenty of time to work him in. Use protective boots or bandages during this period as it is just the time when a silly knock could put you out of action, but don't forget to have someone at hand to take them off and take your stick, if you have one, before starting your test.

Ensure you are correctly dressed for the standard of test and have spurs which are not too long or too sharp and lighter coloured gloves. The whole picture must look neat, tidy and smart. Fly spray should be liberally applied if necessary according to the weather. If there is a tack inspection to see you have the correct bit, spurs and so on, get this over and done with early to avoid upsetting your horse just before going into the arena.

Keep very calm before your test and run it through in your mind a couple of horses before you are due to go. Breathe deeply and keep everything on the slow side, as otherwise you will tend to rush a bit in the heat of the moment.

Common mistakes are usually caused by inexperience or nervousness and, as with everything, it is practice that will overcome most of these. The real secret is relaxation, as the horse is a highly sensitive creature who will quickly pick up any nervous tension on the part of his rider.

Give yourself time to trot quietly round the outside of the arena and listen for the bell to start. Look carefully at the entrance to your arena and approach it, giving yourself plenty of room to get straight before the entry. Handle the horse quietly and take a couple of deep breaths to relax yourself. If the horse will not halt and stand still don't prolong the agony – you have fluffed that movement so just settle down and concentrate on the rest of the test.

Should you be unlucky enough to go wrong and the judge sounds the bell, don't panic (we've all done it at some stage!). Ask where you should restart from and ensure that you know

parked near or under trees or at least open all ramps and windows to allow as much ventilation as possible.

Visit the secretary's tent as soon as possible to collect your number, get a programme and check that there have been no changes to the course. Walk the show jumping course as soon as possible as this phase tends to start early and you get little chance to see the fences unless you do this the day before. Check that you know where your start and finish are and what the bell sounds like to start you. Decide on what studs you will need and put them out ready for use.

# DRESSAGE: JUDGE'S ASSESSMENT

### DRESSAGE TEST

#### Novice standard

The scale of marks is as follows:
10. Excellent
9. Very good
8. Good
7. Fairly good
6. Satisfactory
5. Sufficient
4. Insufficient
3. Fairly bad
2. Bad
1. Very bad
0. Not performed

Approximate Time – 4½ mins

Errors over the course
are penalised:

First Error    2 marks
Second Error    4 marks
Third Error    8 marks
Fourth Error    Elimination

No. *75*    HORSE *Charlie Smithers*    RIDER *Jane Smith*

| | | Test | Max. Marks | Judge's Marks 1 to 10 | Observations |
|---|---|---|---|---|---|
| 1. | A X | Enter at working trot. Halt. Salute. Proceed at working trot | 10 | 6 | Straight entry. Quarters slightly to right on halt |
| 2. | C | Track right | 10 | 7 | |
| 3. | A | Working trot serpentine 3 loops, each loop to go to the side of the arena finishing at C | 10 | 6 | Resisting. Rhythm well maintained |
| 4. | M B BAE | Working canter right. Circle right 20m diameter. Working canter | 10 | 7 | Good to canter |
| 5. | Between E&H K | Half circle right 15m diameter returning to the track between E&K. Working trot | 10 | 7 | |
| 6. | A C | Working trot serpentine 3 loops each loop to go to the side of the arena finishing at C. Working trot | 10 | 8 | |
| 7. | H E EAB | Working canter left. Circle left 20m diameter. Working canter | 10 | 6 | Tossing head |
| 8. | Between B&M F | Half circle left 15m diameter returning to the track between B&F. Working trot | 10 | 6 | Unsteady head |
| 9. | A KXM | Working trot. Change rein and show a few lengthened strides | 10 | 5 | Some attempt |
| 10. | C HXF | Medium walk. Change rein at a free walk on a long rein | 10 | 6 | Pace - could have more compulsion |
| 11. | F A G | Working trot. Down centre line. Halt. Salute. Leave arena at walk on a long rein at A | 10 | 5 | Halt not square behind |
| 12. | | General impression, obedience and calmness | 10 | 7 | Calm & relaxed |
| 13. | | Paces and impulsion | 10 | 6 | Nice rhythm to trot — extension could be more definate |
| 14. | | Position and seat of the rider and correct application of the aids | 10 | 7 | A very sympathetically ridden test - relaxed & calm |
| | | TOTAL | 140 | 89 | |

Total of Column 2 _____

Errors of course _____

Total penalty marks to deduct _____

Total marks to count ___*89*___

Judge's Signature *A Brown* ...............................

# SHOW JUMPING/CROSS-COUNTRY

## QUALITY FIELD

'Cross-country is basically what made me go eventing. I only enjoy riding thoroughbred horses because when you get to the bottom of the tank they always produce a bit more. Through eventing I have met a lot of nice people and had a great deal of fun.' – *Jessica Harrington, Irish national champion*

what you ought to be doing before quietly starting off again, calmly keeping the horse moving forward.

After your final halt at the end of the test, pat your horse and move off on a long rein diagonally out of the arena at the exit at A. You will be eliminated if you do not leave at A and it has happened that in the relief of finishing the test competitors have failed to leave at the correct spot. Don't join this group!

If your horse has gone well take him back to the box. If he has become nervy and you are not happy with his performance, work him round in circles until he settles, so that on your next outing he will start to realize that he must cooperate before he is allowed back to the box for a rest. It may be that you need to adjust the time spent working him in. All horses are different in this respect and need varying amounts to give their best. It is important that you discover what is the optimum time for your horse.

### The show jumping phase

In Britain this usually comes next, before the cross-country, although this may not be the case in other countries. Those who have progressed up through the Pony Club events, where the show jumping is normally last, must also remember to check. The warm up is again very important; start by loosening up on the flat and pop over a small cross pole if possible. The practice area is always a bit of a nightmare, so do be careful that you are not pushed into a situation of frightening your horse off. Allow enough time to have a couple of jumps over both the upright and spread fences, but not necessarily with them set at full height. At this stage your horse just needs a loosen up over the

fences before entering the arena.

Be sure you have the correct hat (one with safety harness) on for jumping and that the chin strap is firmly secured before you start. Give your horse the best possible chance. Canter strongly around the arena, listen for the bell and then perform a nice flowing round. Go steady at planks, gates, uprights and combinations and increase impulsion but keep straight at parallels, triple bars or sloping fences. Remember to maintain the rhythm and ride your corners correctly and you should be on course for a good round.

### The cross-country course

Walking the cross-country course is the most important part of the day. Ideally you should always walk it twice, once to get the feel of it, the second time to decide how and where you are going to jump each fence. Consider the going, the terrain and whether it is flat, hilly or undulating. Establish in your mind where the most difficult fences are situated and whether your horse will be fresh or tired when he gets to them. Go and look at anything you feel unhappy about again; better still, watch someone else go over it and decide from their progress what will be the correct pace and line of approach for your own horse.

Ask yourself what it is you are setting out to achieve on this particular course. Do you need to jump an easier option at an early fence to ensure you have not frightened a young horse before you reach an awkward one later on? Is the ground going to deteriorate later in the day and, if so, what is your alternative plan and line of approach to the combination fences going to be? Are you going out for a win (in which case prepare to take the odd risk to gain some valuable seconds) or is this to be treated as a schooling round, or a confidence giver? Is your horse fit enough – and where in his training programme does this event fall in relation to your ultimate goal? Once you have decided what you want to achieve you now only have to worry about the difficult part of eventing – getting on and doing it.

Look at the start box and how far from the first fence it is. Is it in line? If not, look for the best line to take to reach that obstacle and to give the

A good strong seat is helping this horse to do an impressive and active trot, although the hands could be held slightly more upright. Tweed coats and snaffles are allowed for novice tests.

Coloured horses have enjoyed great popularity as eventers. This one is jumping very neatly in nice style. The rider is looking down which just spoils an otherwise good position over the fence; Janice Bale and Benjamin Little, Pony Club Championships, 1986.

## CROSS-COUNTRY/AFTER CARE

horse a good start. Do not get into the start box too early – it tends to upset the horse. Just walk in and out quietly once and then keep him moving until about 10–15 seconds before you go, then enter it and sit quietly until the count-down. It is often best to turn your mount round to look at the other horses to keep him settled then face forwards as the starter begins the count.

Aim to ride the course in a good steady rhythm. This takes far less out of the horse, although there are times when you may simply have to pull and tug to get at a fence if your horse is on the strong side. Don't forget that your legs are there as a very useful balancing aid and should be used as such on your approach to the fences.

You should make a straight approach to each fence and give the horse the chance of seeing a clear way through. It is amazing the difference that moving a little to the right or left on approaching a fence can make to whether it looks easy or in some cases very difficult. Study the most advantageous point of take off so that you can arrive exactly at that point and feel confident you are giving your horse the best possible ride.

Remember any turning flags out on the course – you must leave red flags to your right and white ones to your left. At the big, straight-forward fences ride on well and at the combinations or very upright ones balance the horse and get his hocks underneath him before expecting him to cope with these neatly. Ride your horse throughout every fence and on, out and round towards the next.

Have plenty of impulsion to cope with coming up the steps or banks on the course and keep riding up to the top and likewise going down – although this is less difficult with most horses so long as you keep them straight.

As you near the end of the course remember that your horse will be tiring a little, so help him along a bit by holding him together a bit more between hand and leg and be very positive at your fences. On finishing, keep a strong feel on the reins and let him gradually pull himself up to a walk. Get off and keep him walking after loosening the girths until he has stopped blowing a lot.

### Care of the horse after the cross-country
This is probably the most important part of the whole event as now is the time he could easily get a chill if you let him stand around too long without moving him. On returning to your truck, take off the saddle and other bits and pieces and wash the horse down quietly and quickly with plenty of water – unless it is a very cold day, in which case keep the water to a minimum. Be careful not to have too much water over the back and loins as this could cause muscle spasm. Scrape off the excess water and take him for a good walk, using a sweat sheet or cooler depending on the weather. Never leave your horse tied up to the truck without a sheet over him unless it is terribly hot – in which case he may be more comfortable back in the lorry out of the sun unless that too has become unbearably hot.

Remove the studs and thoroughly check him over for cuts or bruises and treat as necessary. Offer him small drinks frequently once he has stopped blowing and give him some hay or a small feed.

### The end of the day
At the end of the day your horse must be checked carefully to see that all is well. Is he bandaged, ready to go home? Has he been offered water frequently (especially in hot weather) and is he happy eating his hay and in a relaxed state for the return journey? Have you packed everything up, collected your dressage sheet, thanked organizers, secretary, sponsors and helpers and generally been a good competitor? If so, it is time to start the homeward journey or to take the horse back to his stables to relax, tuck into an appetizing but fairly small feed and settle down for a good and well deserved night's rest.

Washing down the horses after competing is an important part of after care. In cooler weather care has to be taken not to let the horse get chilled.

### TIP FOR THE TOP

'For those of you who want to get your horse to the top, remember that the one-day event is the training ground for the three-day event and should be used as such.' – *Richard Meade, triple Olympic gold medallist*

# THE ULTIMATE TEST

## GETTING THERE

**8**

The three-day event is the pinnacle to which every eventer hopes to aspire one day. Comparatively few manage to achieve their ambition of competing at one, but those that do have the satisfaction of knowing they have reached a standard high enough to warrant their inclusion in the premier division of the eventing league.

There are various standards which affect the height and severity of the course and overall distance. The event is generally held over three days, but at the big international three-day events there are usually two days of dressage to enable the judges to get through the number of starters. The qualifications needed to compete in a three-day event depend very much on the level of event being run. If your ambition is to ride in one it is worth studying these qualifications carefully well in advance to be sure you are planning your programme to include the right number and standard of events to fulfil these entry requirements.

Depending on the event, you will need to allow roughly 12-16 weeks to prepare your horse. This period should include two or three one-day events as part of the build up towards peak fitness.

**Planning ahead**

Careful planning is required when working out how to prepare for your three-day event. Decide first which day you want to arrive, taking into account whether your horse would settle better by arriving a little early to give him time to recover from the journey. The travelling can be considerable in countries such as America and Australia.

Make sure you have arranged for the right type of bedding for your horse. A change just before an event is best avoided if possible, and if you have room it is worth bringing a little extra of your own. Taking enough feed and hay for the duration of your stay needs some careful calculations and you should cater for every eventuality when packing the trunk for your journey. Work out what you need and group items by type. The following checklist may be useful:

1. Feed, hay, water for the journey, bedding, mucking out tools, skips, water buckets × 3 (for washing down as well), feed bins, haynets.

2. Tack – saddles, bridles, girths, breastplates and overgirths, weight cloth and weights, boots, bandages, studs and over reach/bell boots, lead bridle and lead rope on chain, lungeing kit, spares, riding whips, spurs, leather punch, spare set of shoes.

3. Rugs and rollers – night and day wear. Cotton sheets, coolers, towelling rugs or sweat sheets. Towels for use after cross-country, waterproof sheet. Travelling bandages or boots, head collar and rope, tail bandages. Night bandages if necessary.

4. Rider's clothes – hats for all phases, hairnets etc as necessary, coats for dressage and show jumping. Skull cap with appropriate covers for cross-country and show jumping. Cross-country kit including back protector and stop watch. Several pairs of gloves. Stocks and stock pins. Boots and breeches. Exercise clothes.

5. First aid kit (remember that only the official vet can administer any drug) – bandages, cotton wool, under bandage protection, cleansing agent etc, thermometer, dressings, leg and body washes if used. Leg care – kaolin or other poultices, brown paper, plastic, sponges, scrapers and buckets for washing down.

It is always horrifying looking at the kit required but there is nothing worse than discovering too late that you've left some useful item behind. Once you have done a couple of three-day events you will learn what you actually need to take on such an occasion.

**Setting off**

Travelling can take a lot out of the horse, especially if it is very hot or a long and twisty route where the horse rarely relaxes. Decide on the best time of day to travel, and the smoothest route and where you are going to stop to water the horse if it is a long journey. Overnight stops may be necessary if extreme distances are to be covered, so be sure to plan this well in advance. Be careful to check the horse for warmth, as a cold draught on his back throughout the journey will not be the ideal start – but if he is too hot it will take a lot out of him unnecessarily. Motorway journeys are generally cooler for the horse than winding roads and the number of horses

The steeplechase phase is exciting and requires quick reactions. It is considerably faster, hence the shorter stirrups. Steeplechase fences may vary considerably from country to country, but the course itself tends to be either round or a figure of eight shape; Karen Straker and Running Bear, Badminton, 1986.

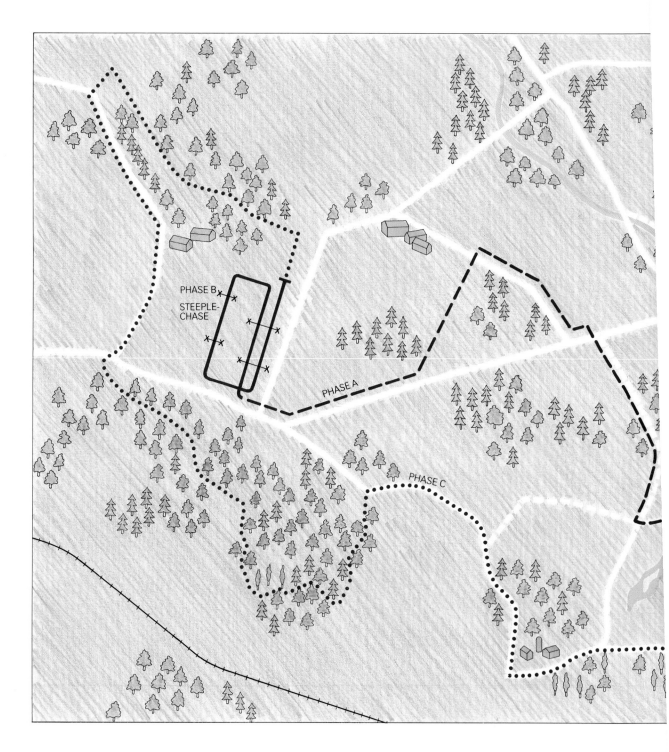

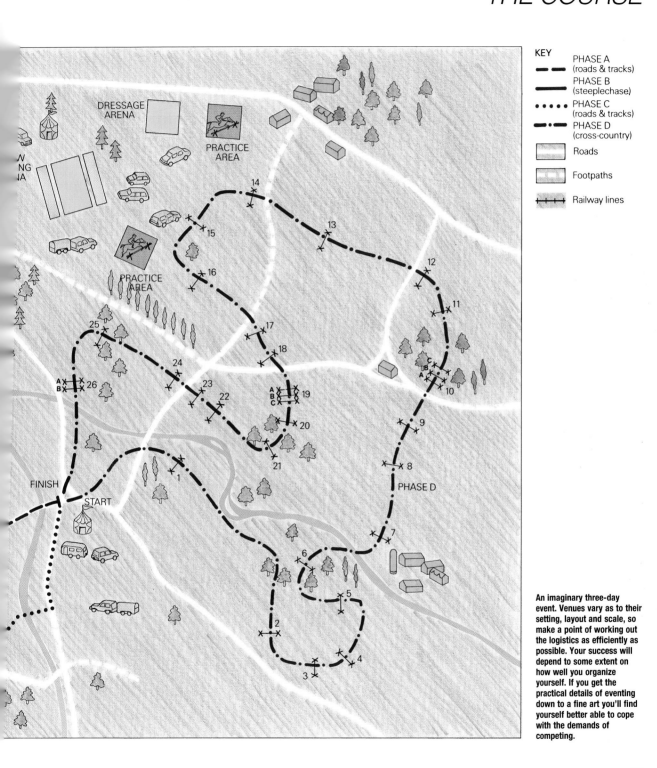

**KEY**

| | |
|---|---|
| PHASE A (roads & tracks) | |
| PHASE B (steeplechase) | |
| PHASE C (roads & tracks) | |
| PHASE D (cross-country) | |
| Roads | |
| Footpaths | |
| Railway lines | |

DRESSAGE ARENA

PRACTICE AREA

PRACTICE AREA

FINISH

START

PHASE D

An imaginary three-day event. Venues vary as to their setting, layout and scale, so make a point of working out the logistics as efficiently as possible. Your success will depend to some extent on how well you organize yourself. If you get the practical details of eventing down to a fine art you'll find yourself better able to cope with the demands of competing.

# THE ULTIMATE TEST
## ARRIVAL/VETERINARY INSPECTION

travelling together can also make a difference. It may be necessary to start with thicker rugs and then take something off as the day warms up.

Some people travel their horse with a small haynet, others without. I always travel with one if the horse is not competing within four hours, as I believe that it is more relaxing for them to be able to pick at a bit of hay as they go along. The greedy horse may need to be given only a small amount.

Make sure the horse is well protected for the journey. The vulnerable spots are usually knees, hocks, tails and hips, so study how your horse stands in the truck to check if any of these are likely to suffer, especially if you have to brake suddenly. Travelling boots are quick and easy but do not give the support of bandages; however, badly put on bandages may do untold damage if left on for a long time with uneven pressure or with the tapes tied too tight.

### Arrival
On arrival take your flu vaccinations, passport and any other forms that may have been asked for to the stabling manager or whoever you have been told to report to. Find out where you are stabled, where the horsebox is to be parked and any other relevant information. Go and check the stable and ensure that there is enough bedding, and find out where the water is situated and where best to unload.

Lead your horse around for a few minutes to let him loosen up after the journey, then put him in his stable. Remove the main travelling kit and leave him with hay and water to settle quietly into his new surroundings while you sort everything out, clean out the horsebox and generally get organized for the next few days.

Your helper is especially important at a three-day event as he or she will be left alone quite a lot

while you re-walk the course and so on. It is best to sit down together each day and plan how you are going to do everything and what times you want to meet up and ride throughout the event. Check that the accommodation, washing and catering facilities are all right if you are staying somewhere different and that he or she has plenty of money and bedding. Grooms are often not very well looked after at three-day events, which are tiring and hectic, so do make sure yours has the best possible conditions.

### The veterinary inspections
The first veterinary inspection usually takes place the afternoon before the dressage starts, after which declarations to start the event close. If you present your horse at the vets' inspection you are generally considered a starter, but check through the event information to be sure you don't have to declare at any other time. You should be ready for it in plenty of time, with your horse spotlessly clean, plaited and wearing a bridle. You should be dressed neatly and tidily. Many people take their horses for a hack before this first stage of the competition, but if you do keep his legs well protected in case of a knock, especially with so many horses milling around. Keep a hoofpick handy to pick out your horse's feet before running him up in case he has picked up mud or a stone when walking around.

When it is your turn (don't be late or you will be eliminated) walk your horse up in front of the inspection panel and stand in front of him so that they can look at him. Walk him away straight and carefully, turn him (push him away from you to do this) and trot him back and on past the panel. Keep his head straight – if it is turned in towards you he may do some uneven steps – and you must be prepared to run fast if he is a freegoing mover. You should have practised your run up in hand several times at home. Difficult horses may be best run up in a coupling and lead rein, and you should carry a stick.

The second of the compulsory inspections comes on Day 2 of the competition, at the end of the second round of roads and tracks (Phase C). There is a fenced off section (the 'box') that you enter on completing the course where the inspection takes place. You should trot straight towards the inspection panel until you are

There are two veterinary inspections on the second day of a three-day competition, before and after the cross-country phases. How well a horse copes with a competition will depend on his level of fitness, despite factors like the weather, the severity of the course and its length. The vets will not allow a horse to continue which does not appear fit to do so; David Green and Count de Bolebec, Burghley 1987.

through the finish. They will then usually ask you to dismount as they look over your horse, watch his breathing and test his heart rate and sometimes temperature in hot and humid conditions. Provided they are satisfied, you can then get on with washing down and refreshing your horse during this vital period. If there is a problem – which is quite rare – they will advise you. Never forget, however, that the inspection panel are professionals and, although they would hate to stop you completing the course, if they think your horse would suffer from continuing they will do so. It is much better that way than wrecking your horse for good.

At the last inspection on the last day, before the show jumping, it is vital that your horse has been well loosened up. A good quarter of an hour's walking, followed by some trotting and cantering, should do the trick, but do not tire the horse unnecessarily after his exertions of the previous day. Once loosened, keep him walking and if he is lazy have your groom positioned to chase him up when you go in front of the panel.

### Assessing the course

When you exercise your horse after arriving rather depends on what is happening during the rest of the day. There will at some stage be a briefing about the course, followed by a conducted tour of the roads and tracks, steeplechase and cross country courses. The briefing is your chance to learn any useful tips on what should and should not be done during the event. You will find out where to exercise, where to collect numbers, any relevant up-to-date news on the course, going, flagging of fences, route to the steeplechase for helpers and so on, and this is the main chance for you to ask any questions if necessary. Take a note book and

### IRISH PROBLEM

'The Irish have contributed greatly to the eventing scene. We give horses a great start in the hunting field – once they've done that they'll go anywhere. Being a country of sellers, all our best horses go abroad.' – *Van der Vater, veteran Irish international rider*

pen with you. Immediately afterwards a conducted tour around the roads and tracks shows you the route, flagged check points (which must be passed through under penalty of elimination) and the various kilometre markers. Note down the markers on your event map and the ground conditions between each kilometre marker, as this may determine your pace between each. Later, when you work out your times (generally allowing 4 minutes per kilometre), you may decide that one kilometre requires 5 minutes because it includes a rough stretch, while another across good open land only needs 3 minutes.

The steeplechase course (usually between 1 and 2 miles) may be a round course or the more favoured figure of eight type which includes a couple of changes of rein. You walk this on foot and should look at your approach into each fence as, with the extra speed, you will arrive at them considerably quicker than normal. Look carefully at your turns and how best to ride round them. Although in theory it is best to hug the rails, sometimes a turn will be easier by going a little wide at the start and then coming in closer at the end of the bend to get your best line. Think which is the horse's best side and which perhaps may prove more difficult for him. Be sure the route is absolutely clear in your mind if you have to do two circuits, as your first circuit may not include going through the finish first time round but going via a separate channel. Be absolutely sure what you are meant to do on the first and last circuit, as even top competitors have eliminated themselves by not checking this thoroughly enough.

Walking the cross-country course for a three-day event is no different in essence from walking it for a one-day event. No doubt you'll be a dab hand at it by now (see p. 59)! However, it is worth remembering that at this level you will be coming up against first class horses and riders whose fitness and aptitude will be proven, so you cannot afford to be less than thorough in your assessment of the course. (This point applies, of course, to the roads and tracks and steeplechase elements too.) You should make a note of each fence and the difficulty it presents. Identify stretches of the course that need extra care and those that will enable you to push on

and save or make up time. Make sure that you assess correctly what the going demands and have noted any hidden pitfalls in the shape of rabbit holes, tree roots or overhanging branches. An accurate mental picture of the course will not only give you confidence, but will make you more purposeful and better able to cope with the hazards that lie ahead.

## THE DRESSAGE PHASE

The first day of competition is taken up with the dressage tests. Most people tend to ride their horses in well before their tests and then go back to the stable for a while and have a major tidy up before appearing about 15–30 minutes before they are scheduled to perform.

The atmosphere at a three-day event may affect your horse and he may need considerably more work than usual. Don't forget that he is now at peak fitness, so allow yourself plenty of time to work him well should this be necessary. A good dressage test makes all the difference, and will leave you less to make up on the cross-country the next day.

In most events there will be a tack inspection, so find out who is doing this and get checked early so that there is no last minute rush to upset your horse. Make quite certain that your tack is legal. The permitted saddlery is clearly stated in your rule book and any queries should have

**Lucinda Green's Shannagh seems rather bored by the final tidy up before the dressage. A 'bun', false or otherwise, with a top hat and tails is correct dress for tests at Advanced or International level; Stockholm, 1987.**

# THE ULTIMATE TEST

## WEIGHING-OUT/BACK-UP

**Securing the bridle to the top plait by means of a shoelace will ensure that it stays in place should you slip off over the horse's head. It's bad enough falling off, but to be left holding the bridle with no horse is disastrous!**

been clarified at the briefing. Remember that dressage is a visual art, so present yourself looking spotless with an immaculately groomed horse all set to do your very best. If your horse starts to hot up keep him moving quietly and either work him harder or adopt a relaxed attitude to help him settle. Before entering the arena check that his boots and your whip have been removed and prepare yourself to go out in front of the judges to do the very best you can.

### THE SECOND DAY

The second day of the competition is by far the heaviest in its demands of horse and rider. Called the speed and endurance phase it has four elements, to be completed in the following sequence: roads and tracks, first phase (2–3 miles); steeplechase (1–2 miles); roads and tracks, second phase (3–6 miles); and the cross-country (2½–4½ miles).

The timing of your preparations on the second day will depend on when you are due to compete. Feed your horse and remove his hay at least four hours before your start time. If he is likely to eat his bedding tie him up or put on a muzzle if he is used to one. In hot weather be sure to offer regular drinks up to an hour before, but do not let him have more than a quarter of a bucket at a time. If you go late in the day he can be led out to graze in the morning and possibly given a small feed up to four hours before your start time.

Keep your horse calm and avoid fussing him unnecessarily; he has a busy time ahead so requires some peace and quiet. At some stage plait his top plait and thread a shoelace through. This can be secured round the bridle headpiece to keep it in place should the rider fall and be in danger of pulling the bridle off (see illustration above). Some people plait for cross-country but I like to have the mane to grab hold of in emergency! Put in studs according to the ground conditions (see illustrations on page 47) and put on bandages or boots not more than half an hour before the start time. Over-reach boots should also be put on.

### Weighing out

Above novice level three-day events it is compulsory to carry weights on the second day of the competition. There is a mandatory weighing-out before the start, so make sure that you are dressed and ready in plenty of time for this. You will need to take all your tack plus a weight cloth if you are not likely to make the minimum permitted weight of 165lb (75kg). The bridle is not used, but can be claimed on weighing-in at the end if you are underweight. The formalities out of the way, it is now time to concentrate on preparing for the 'off'.

### Back-up

Choose a spot to put all your kit, preferably not too close to everyone else's. Sometimes this is very difficult so it is best to reserve your place early by putting at least water, buckets and sponges down. If possible choose a shady place, as the secret of the 10-minute halt, which comes at the end of the second phase of roads and tracks, is to cool and refresh your horse ready for the cross-country, without unduly worrying him. The following is a list of the equipment that you should have to hand at the box to cover any problems which may arise.

1. Water – this should be provided but check first
2. Buckets, sponges, scrapers for washing down
3. Coolers, sweat sheet, rug, waterproof, depending on the weather

4. Spare set of shoes and studs in case shoe is lost
5. Spare bridle and other tack, especially leathers, in case anything breaks
6. Towels for drying horse off
7. Spare boots or bandages in case of damage
8. Spare set of over-reach boots
9. Spare whip and gloves for rider
10. Warm jacket if cold
11. Drink for rider

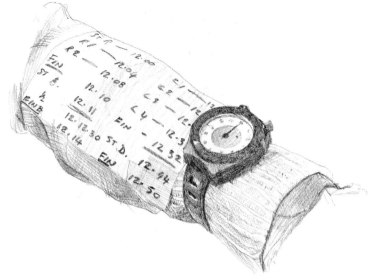

## Roads and tracks

The horse will not need any warm up as this first round of tracks and roads acts as a substitute, so it is not necessary to mount more than a few minutes before the start. Have your groom bring the horse to the start box at a pre-arranged time. The start may not be in the same area as the main 'box' so make sure you arrange to meet at the right place. Finally, check that you have got your number, whip, gloves and spurs and everything that is necessary to send you on your way.

Timing is very important in the three-day event. It is worth taking a spare stop watch. I set my watch 5 minutes before the start at 5 minutes before the hour, which makes calculations much simpler should there be a delay at some stage during the day. Double-check your watch just before the start. When the signal comes, set off at a brisk trot, pressing the stopwatch button as you go.

## The steeplechase

Try to complete the first phase of roads and tracks with time to spare before the steeplechase, finishing perhaps 1½–2 minutes before your start time. This phase requires a sharp eye, firm leg contact, a good grip and the ability to ride like a jump jockey. You'll be riding harder into the fences than you do for the cross-country and at extra speed, so it is vital that your helper should examine girths, studs and generally look over your equipment before proceeding to the only place you may receive assistance on the course, the check area, which is about 100 yards from the finish. Most riders don't stop at this point, but your groom should check that all shoes are in place and all seems well for the second phase of roads and tracks.

## The 10-minute halt

You'll come off Phase C (second phase of roads and tracks) at the 'box' where you will have to present your horse for a veterinary inspection. There is a 10-minute halt between Phase C and Phase D (the cross-country) which allows you time to refresh your horse and yourself for the last but most crucial element of the second day. It is most important that you use these valuable few minutes to best advantage.

Follow the example of professional eventers at the 10-minute halt and exert yourself as little as possible. Once the horse has been checked by the vets, wash him down well and scraper him off. Check shoes and studs, keep him walking and if it is cold keep him warm without overheating. It is not vital to remove the saddle but loosen the girths and, when retightening them, be sure to pull the weight cloth well up into the front arch of the saddle (see illustration on page 76). Grease down the front of the horse's hind legs, particularly over the hocks and fetlock joints, and check that your chin strap is done up and that your whip and gloves have been collected. Mount 2 minutes before the start to give yourself time to wake the horse up again. Enter the start box when called and be ready to go immediately the starter gives the signal.

**Most riders write their target times on a piece of paper and attach it to their arm for easy reading. The stop watch is essential for accuracy, so always carry a spare – and don't forget to press the button as you start!**

# THE ULTIMATE TEST

An anxious rider during the countdown to the cross-country. The role of the groom and helpers is to refresh and relax the horse and inform and, if possible, calm the rider at this nerve-wracking stage of a three-day event; Burghley, 1987.

# THE ULTIMATE TEST
## END OF THE CROSS-COUNTRY/FINAL PHASE

**The weight cloth should always be pulled well up into the front arch of the saddle before tightening the girths so that the weight does not press down on the horse's withers.**

### The end of the cross-country
At the end of the cross-country the rider must first weigh-in and then the horse is briefly checked by the inspection panel. Keep the horse walking quietly for a few moments before washing him off, being careful over the loin area. Keep him walking for half an hour after this, but be sure he will not get cold if the weather is chilly. Allow him to have short sips of water as soon as he has stopped puffing, with electrolytes if necessary every 15 minutes until he is satisfied. His legs will have required soaping to remove the dirt and grease and should have been carefully checked over for injury. Bandage them for comfort and support, either dry or with an appropriate medication, and leave him to relax. Some horses might want a *small* feed as soon as you have settled them, others it is best to leave just with hay until later.

After a few hours' rest lead your horse out, walk him around to ease stiffness and jog up to see if he is sound. Some will be quite stiff, others hardly at all, but if there are any worries call the duty vet who will advise at any time. Leave the horse to rest as much as possible and give him a warm, smallish, nutritious feed, with electrolytes in his water if necessary, to settle him for the evening. This is not the time for bran mashes — the horse still has another day to do. Check him regularly and be sure he is quite comfortable and warm. If he breaks out in a sweat and his ears are cold, walk him out and rub his ears gently to warm him up.

### THE FINAL PHASE
Be up early the next morning, check his legs and lead him out to see how he is. If there are any problems, call the vet to see how you should proceed. If all seems well he can be plaited and then loosened up in time for the final veterinary check.

### Show jumping
Before the show jumping walk your course carefully, remembering that normally you can only do this when you are correctly dressed for the competition.

Sometimes there is a parade of all competitors so be ready for this and, depending on when you are due to jump, loosen your horse up gradually in trot and canter. He will be stiff, so give him time to loosen up before jumping a few practice fences. He will not feel quite the same as in a one-day event so don't overdo it. He needs loosening, not tiring, before doing the show jumping, but he must be woken up and ready to go on entering the arena.

### After the event
On completion of the event you will hopefully have received a prize and have the satisfaction of finishing all three days. Remember to thank the organizers, stable manager and officials and leave your stable clean and tidy. Most people tend to leave that evening, so settle your horse and bandage him carefully. Some sort of leg medication may be advisable, especially if it is a long journey. Keep him warm and if possible give him a small feed before the trip.

The care after the event is just as important as that before. He will need to rest both mentally and physically and will require a letting-down period when the energy food intake should be decreased and he can be given more fattening foods. Hacking out quietly or turning out with leg protection for 2–3 hours a day is best for the first week, before either letting him right down for a couple of months or letting him half down for a certain period, when turning out and occasional quiet hacks may be best depending on your plans for the future.

The winner's lap of honour. Only a few will experience this moment of triumph, but it's the participating rather than the winning which is sufficient for so many eventers around the world. Ian Stark decided that this was not enough and set out to fulfil his ambition of winning Badminton. He did – on Sir Wattie in 1986.

# AFTERTHOUGHTS

Sometimes I ask myself why we all enjoy our eventing so much and find there is no simple answer. On the down side there are those awful moments when the dressage has been horrendous — once for me it was even worse! The horse took off out of the arena on seeing a herd of deer emerge over the brow of a nearby hill and there was no way I could get it anywhere near let alone back in to complete my test. I was eliminated, of course. On another occasion, after a good test and a supposedly brilliant clear round in the show jumping, I heard the announcer give out that I was eliminated for missing out the last fence. I'd watched an earlier competitor round the course and then dashed off to warm up, but had failed to hear that he'd been eliminated for missing the last. The moral is — if you are unable to walk the course, watch another competitor go right round the course and actually through the finish. Never make assumptions.

All sorts of dramas tend to happen on the cross-country, especially with horses that are a bit green and over the years I've experienced most of them: been out of control, missed fences, gone out through the start in the wrong direction, knocked over flags, judges, dogs, children, and once I jumped out over a car after failing to negotiate a sharp turn. The falls have been too numerous to mention, but it's no fun landing on the ground first and seeing your horse's hooves — into which you have so carefully screwed some rather lethal looking studs — fast descending towards your limp body. Thoughts of self preservation flash through your mind and mingle with such silly ideas as wills, paying your debts, feeling sorry you snapped someone's head off just before you set off, etc, etc. But from somewhere comes a nagging message to awaken a response that has been drilled into you: "Don't just lie there. Get up and finish the course." Somehow you do despite the aches and pains — which you rarely notice until you've finished!

On the plus side there is nothing better than to complete a course on a horse you know, enjoy and understand; particularly so if you've done it on a horse you've brought on yourself or nurtured through a difficult time and had the satisfaction of rebuilding his confidence.

It gives one a tremendous thrill and sense of achievement to finish a three-day event after a build up of months to get there. The ultimate, of course, is to win. That's what we all aim for. I've been lucky enough to have won a few times over the years and with many wonderful horses. I hope that all those who read this book may be equally as fortunate and enjoy their events as much as I have.

Jane Holderness-Roddam, 1988

# INDEX